THE SCRATCH
& SNIFF
GUIDE TO
BEER

Published in 2017 by Harper Design
An Imprint of HarperCollinsPublishers
195 Broadway
New York, NY 10007
Tel: (212) 207-7000
Fax: (855) 746-6023
harperdesign@harpercollins.com
www.hc.com

Distributed throughout
North America by
HarperCollins Publishers
195 Broadway
New York, NY 10007

First Published in 2017 by Quintet,
an imprint of The Quarto Group.
The Old Brewery, 6 Blundell Street,
London N7 9BH, United Kingdom.
T (0)20 7700 6700 F (0)20 7700 8066
www.QuartoKnows.com

Quintet Publishing Team:
ART DIRECTOR: Karen Hood
DESIGNER: Ginny Zeal
COVER DESIGN: Wide Open Studio
MANAGING EDITOR: Rica Dearman
SENIOR EDITOR: Caroline Elliker
EDITORIAL DIRECTOR: Emma Bastow
PUBLISHER: Mark Searle

ISBN 978-0-06-269148-4

Library of Congress Control
Number 2017932206

First printing 2017

Printed in China

THE SCRATCH & SNIFF GUIDE TO BEER

A BEER LOVER'S COMPANION

Justin Kennedy

Foreword by Rich Higgins
Master Cicerone®

HARPER DESIGN
An Imprint of HarperCollins Publishers

CONTENTS

GET STARTED
WITH SCRATCH AND SNIFF ON PAGE 15

Turn to page 15 to discover the delights of the ten scratch-and-sniff stickers in this book. Simply touch the sticker (no scratching required, these days!) to release the unique scent relevant to the page you are reading. Sniff, and enjoy!

FOREWORD

Recent, informal polls taken by me suggest that there are two primary reasons to drink beer: 1. Beer is fun! 2. Beer is delicious!

Given these two important aspects of beer, the amazing book in your hands has to do with a third aspect: the more you learn about beer, the more fun and delicious it becomes. I'm not going to say that the unexamined beer is not worth drinking, but it sure is less inspiring, fun, and delicious.

For example, should you find yourself in a biergarten (which I recommend), you might order a German wheat beer (which I also recommend). With each hearty sip, you're drinking a great beer. If you don't know anything more about the beer, that's okay, but I guess that's that: good beer; but not much of a highlight reel.

Let *The Scratch & Sniff Guide to Beer* tell you about that beer you're drinking, and the beer will get better, sip by sip and page by page. This book's an easy approach to becoming a well-informed beer drinker. In-depth tasting of a beer is basically a drink-and-sniff operation, so this ingenious scratch-and-sniff book offers some vital practice.

Once you know where your wheat beer is brewed, it can transport you. Maybe it's brewed at a monastery in the foothills of the Alps. You can imagine a satisfied monk, sipping that beer while gazing out at snow-capped peaks on the horizon. Not bad. This beer just got more interesting.

And what if you know that the yeast that fermented this weissbier creates fruity flavors in

the beer? You'll then be able to peg that fruity flavor of ripe banana that makes German weissbier so surprisingly, beguilingly delicious.

Sitting in your biergarten, sipping your weissbier, you might get hungry. But before you start looking to complement your beer with a banana split, think instead about what Bavarians like to eat. Believe it or not, that banana flavor is actually a ninja trained to sneak you the flavor antidote to sausages, smoked pork, onions, and mustard. (Try it for yourself. It's *sehr gut!*)

Now, with *The Scratch & Sniff Guide to Beer* in hand and armed with a little knowledge of beer history, geography, science, and food pairing, I'd be willing to bet your weissbier (or your pilsner, IPA, rauchweizenbock, or what have you) is more delicious and your visit to the biergarten is more fun. (Not down with weissbier? No problem. The book covers a zillion other beer styles, too.)

In my years of professional brewing, beer teaching, and beer travel, I'm constantly amazed at beer and the amount of stuff there is to learn, taste—and sniff! This book is the perfect place to start your journey toward enjoying beer even more than you thought you could.

A little beer is delicious. A little curiosity makes beer more inspiring. And a little knowledge allows beer to take you places. *Cheers!*

RICH HIGGINS, *MASTER CICERONE*®
SAN FRANCISCO, CALIFORNIA June 2017

INTRO

One of the most common questions I get as an active player in this beer-writing business is: "What's your favorite beer?" It has no simple answer. That's because my favorite beer changes all the time. Being someone who is often constantly surrounded by a vast selection of great pilsners, IPAs, and saisons, my "favorite beer" depends on any number of factors or circumstances.

Throw me into a summertime backyard with a gaggle of friends, a charcoal grill, and a platter of burgers and hot dogs, and my favorite beer is the coldest can of pale lager I find at the bottom of an ice cooler.

Put me in front of a fireplace-equipped cabin in the middle of the Catskill Mountains and my favorite beer is something dark and roasty with a whiff of smoke and a boozy, warming finish.

Some people are more finicky, having a single favorite beer no matter what the situation. And that's okay! But the reality is many of us are faced with a plethora of beer choices on a regular basis, and it takes a lot of work to navigate them. This book aims to do just that in a cursory but fun way—it's packed with beer intel, but it isn't encyclopedic. It covers most of the bases, but not all the minutiae. It's a book about beers that are interesting and historic, with fun graphics, puzzles, and aromatic stickers to lighten the mood and pull back the curtain on a subject that consumers find increasingly daunting and complicated.

Before we get into the meat, er . . . malt, of the matter, let's talk a little about history and process.

Bison Beer Crafthouse bottle store, Brighton, UK

A BRIEF HISTORY OF BEER

Beer was born of necessity. It organically evolved as a means of transforming readily available ingredients into cellar-stable, easily digestible calories. It was a preservation method, a sanitary form of hydration, and pure, potable liquid sustenance. It's often argued that the invention of bread and beer are at least partially responsible for the birth of civilization and the development of technology—a bold claim, but not entirely far-fetched.

So ingrained was beer consumption in the ancient world that its name derives from the Latin *bibere*, meaning simply "to drink." But fermented grain beverages go back well beyond that. The Babylonians had recipes for it and the workers who built the Egyptian pyramids practically survived on—and some say were paid in—beer. One of the earliest written beer recipes—etched into clay tablets—is the *Hymn to Ninkasi*, a song praising the Sumerian goddess of beer and alcohol that doubles as a guide to brewing beer:

Ancient Egypt pyramid building

The potable drink spread wherever imperialism and trade routes took it, eventually flourishing in places where grain was abundant and available for much of the year. The ingredients varied from region to region, and were often made with whatever grains were on hand—rice, millet, barley, maize, or any number of other fermentable sugars—as well as botanicals like bittering herbs, flowers, roots, and branches.

By the 1500s, German beer had become what we think of it as today—a malted barley-based beverage brewed with water and bittered with hops. This base formula resulted from the so-called beer purity law, or *Reinheitsgebot*, which regulated what could and could not be used in brewing beer.

Today, beer varieties are vast and complicated, but can be broken down very broadly into two overarching categories: ales and lagers. There's often more than a little overlap, and many dozens of subcategories exist.

Hymn to Ninkasi

You are the one who soaks the malt in a jar...

You are the one who spreads
the cooked mash on large reed mats...

You are the one who holds with
both hands the great sweet wort...

When you pour out the filtered
beer of the collector vat, It is like the
onrush of Tigris and Euphrates...

HOW IT'S BREWED

Beer is an extremely easy beverage to make. All it takes is some water, a little grain, a bittering agent, and time. Many people throughout the world do it at home and achieve respectable results without a ton of effort.

Making *good* beer though? Now, that's another story. Not only is maintaining consistency from brew to brew extremely difficult, but having so many variables that influence a beer's flavors creates hazards and roadblocks throughout the entire brewing and fermentation process.

At its very basic, beer is made with just four ingredients: yeast, water, hops, and malt. (Some would argue—*accurately*—that beer doesn't have to include hops; although true, there must be some bittering agent to balance the malty backbone and act as a preservative.) Many beers contain way more than four ingredients—fruits, sugars, and other adjuncts—but regardless of how many go in, the process of brewing it is basically the same.

First, hot water is added to malted grain to extract sugars. This step is known as the mash and it happens in a vessel called the mash tun. Every brewery uses a different mashing process, but it usually steeps for around an hour at 150°F. The spent grains are then filtered out and the resulting sweet mixture is called the wort, which is transferred to a brew kettle.

The wort is boiled for an extended time and hops are added at various stages. The hops generate bitterness and provide preservative qualities. Those added near the end of the boil, during what's called the whirlpool phase, impart big, hoppy aromas.

Yeast

Water

Hops

Malt

The four ingredients of beer

THE BEER-MAKING
PROCESS

Behold the fundamental steps that breweries take, and the equipment they use, when producing beer...

Malt

Milling

Mashing

Lautering

Hops

Boiling

Yeast

Fermentation

Cooling

Whirlpool

Beer tank

Packaging

Distribution

The beer is then chilled and sent to a large (usually) stainless-steel tank called a fermentation vessel (FV for short). Brewer's yeast is added, which immediately gets to work converting the wort's sugars and starches into alcohol, carbon dioxide, and other flavors and aromatic compounds. Depending on the type of beer being made, the species of yeast will work at either warm temperatures (ale) or cooler temperatures (lager). Ales usually take about three weeks to ferment, while lagers take much longer, around five or six weeks.

Once the beer is finished fermenting, it's time for packaging. But first the beer is transferred to yet another vessel, called a brite beer tank, where it rests before going into kegs, bottles, or cans and is ready to hit the market.

NOW, IT'S TIME TO DRINK. PROST!

TOP THREE BEERS CONSUMED WHILE WRITING THIS BOOK

As the saying goes, it takes a lot of beer to write about beer. Here are the top three beers I drank while working on this book. Rest assured, I enjoyed every drop.

1. EVIL TWIN MOLOTOV LITE IMPERIAL IPA
2. THREES BREWING VLIET PILSNER
3. CARTON BOAT BEER

Carton Brewing Company's Boat Beer

HOW TO USE THIS BOOK: A ROAD MAP TO SCRATCH-AND-SNIFF

Before we embark on our exciting adventure in beer, here's a lowdown on what you can expect to find in the pages ahead...

This book is much more than your average story of beer. The scratch-and-sniff stickers scattered throughout will reward you with unique aromas that will ensure your reading experience is extra special. We've deliberately kept things fresh and reverent by sticking to beer styles that are concurrently historic and popular at this moment in time. See page 15 for more information on where the stickers are, and how they work.

Meanwhile, the first part of the book (pages 16–31) focuses on important European beer styles—pilsners, porters, saisons, and lambics—followed by aggressive New World styles (pages 32–47) based on the hoppy ales of the US—think IPAs and imperial stouts.

We then dive into two of the four main ingredients that make modern beer what it is: hops and grain. We explore six geographic regions where hops are grown and look at the most important varieties (pages 48–67). The grain chapter (pages 68–81) discusses how and why grains are processed for beer production, and we also look at lesser-known malts like rye, oats, corn, and rice.

Pages 82–97 offer practical tips for purchasing, storing, and serving beer, followed by a chapter on pairing beer and food (pages 98–117), along with a handful of recipes for cooking with beer. We then turn our attention to beer label artwork—one of the most important aspects of selling beer in an increasingly crowded marketplace (pages 118–129). We end our journey with a chapter on beer-themed travel (pages 130–145), including Beer Quests in three distinct geographic regions.

Finally, you'll also discover a few puzzles and "raves"—short commentaries on beers, styles, ingredients, or personalities of note. Enjoy!

Prepare to go on a beautiful journey through the world of beer, with the help of the folks at Bison Beer Crafthouse, Brighton, UK, whose trained experts chose the unique sticker scents throughout this book

FIND THE SCRATCH AND SNIFF STICKERS IN THIS BOOK

You'll notice a scattering of scratch-and-sniff stickers throughout this book. These provide a sensory blast of the flavors and aromas discussed on the page they appear on. Although the stickers say scratch and sniff, you have the option to either scratch or touch and sniff to release the scent.

HOPS
FRONT COVER
One of the key ingredients of beer!

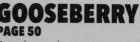
GOOSEBERRY
PAGE 50
Gooseberry is a common aroma in American hops

CLOVE
PAGE 24
Tripels can be spicy and redolent of clove

CEDAR
PAGE 55
A fresh cedar aroma is found in Northern Brewer

DRIED FRUIT
PAGE 30
Barleywines have sweet aromas of dried fruit

DEMERARA SUGAR **PAGE 69**
Malts caramelize to produce a sweet aroma

PINE
PAGE 34
American IPAs contain notes of pine

WHISKEY
PAGE 88
Beer can be stored in barrels that once held whiskey

GRAPEFRUIT
PAGE 47
American barleywines can have grapefruit aromas

CHARCUTERIE
PAGE 117
Smoky, peaty ales pair well with meat

THE CLASSICS

To kick things off, we'll first explore traditional classic beer styles from Belgium, Germany, and the UK.

The world of beer styles can be divided into any number of categories—light versus dark, Old World versus New World—but the most common way to split them is into ales and lagers. Ales are the ancients of the industry, while lagers—despite their modern market dominance—are the vanguard.

Today, light lager accounts for more than 90 percent of all beer produced around the world.

Light lager, the world's most popular beer

PILSNERS AND LAGERS

The underlying difference between ales and lagers is the type of yeast used to ferment the beer.

Lagers are fermented under cool temperatures, around 45 to 55°F, while ales ferment at warmer temperatures, around 65 to 75°F. Ale yeasts work much faster than lagering, which requires a secondary rest. Indeed, the word "lager" itself comes from *lagern*, the German word for "storing."

After the primary fermentation is complete, lagers undergo a prolonged cold-temperature rest, resulting in a clean, crisp, and nuanced flavor. Ales are typically fruity and aromatic by comparison. (The two categories are basically distinct, but occasionally cross streams in certain instances, like Baltic porters and California steam beers.)

Lagers' global dominance began in mid-nineteenth-century central Europe with the invention of refrigeration and cold transport. They include myriad styles like bocks, Märzens, and dunkels, but the king of lagers is the pilsner.

While most people think of pilsner as a German style, it has roots across the border in the Bohemian town of Plzeň, now part of the Czech Republic. The nineteenth-century breweries of Plzeň wanted a superior lager to call their own and commissioned a Bavarian brewer named Josef Groll to construct a recipe based on the German lagers of Bavaria.

The twist was Groll's Plzeň recipe incorporated local ingredients—namely Moravian barley and aromatic Saaz hops. The style was like Bavarian lagers, but had gentler, more nuanced aromas and a crisp, clean taste, making it an uber-easy drinker. The original Bohemian pilsner, Pilsner Urquell, is still around today after nearly 175 years, with Groll's original recipe basically intact.

German pilsners, on the other hand, are arguably more popular today than ever, and they often eclipse their Bohemian ancestors with name recognition and a more robust worldwide distribution. They're distinguished by a pronounced hop bitterness resulting from German-grown bittering hops that are more aggressively biting than the Saaz variety.

A common global misconception is that all lagers are pale and watery. In fact, the world of lagers is as diverse and varied as that of ales. Many are rich and complex, while others are dry and roasty. They vary from the straw-hued pilsners of Bohemia to the black schwarzbiers of central Germany. Other examples include the mild Vienna lagers of Austria; the malty, strong bocks of Einbeck; and the dark but refreshing dunkels of Munich.

*TRY: **PILSNER URQUELL, AYINGER OKTOBER FEST-MÄRZEN, EINBECKER BRAUHERREN PILS, KÖSTRITZER SCHWARZBIER***

REINHEITSGEBOT

For non-Germans, perhaps the most misunderstood beer concept is the *Reinheitsgebot*, or "German Beer Purity Law." In general, the law dictated beer be made with three ingredients only: water, malted barley, and hops. (Yeast was added recently, after a better understanding of microbiology emerged.) Today, there are two versions of the law: a more restrictive one for Bavaria and a laxer one for the rest of Germany. The modern Bavarian law says brewers must use exactly four ingredients for lagers: hops, water, malt, and yeast. Outside Bavaria, additional ingredients may be used (e.g., added sugars). (Slightly different rules apply to ales.) Parts of the law were struck down by the European Court in 1987 for unfairly restricting free trade, but today brewers making beer for domestic sale in Germany must comply with the *Reinheitsgebot*.

THE ORIGINAL INDIA PALE ALE

India pale ale (IPA) is one of the most popular and mythologized beer styles in the world. And though small American producers get due credit for its recent revival and newfound popularity, its origins date back to late-eighteenth-century England.

Legend has it that the very first IPAs were brewed strong with a surplus of hops and alcohol as preservatives to sustain it during the wild seafaring journey from London to colonial India. But similar beers were already popular decades before they were routinely shipped to India.

Never mind that many other styles were shipped to India, too, but they didn't gain the folkloric status ascribed to the almighty IPA. By the mid-nineteenth century, pale ales were encroaching on dark ales' dominance as the go-to beer style of England. But their reign didn't last long. By the twentieth century, even lighter German-style lagers were gaining global momentum and IPA's popularity declined. British brewers developed a new breed of lower-ABV, less aggressively hopped pale ales to compete.

Meanwhile, across the Atlantic, traditional Burton-on-Trent-style British IPA production was preserved with beers like New Jersey's Ballantine IPA, which found an American audience of eager imbibers. That soon fizzled too with the enactment of Prohibition and a continued global distaste for strong ales. By the 1970s, IPA was all but forgotten worldwide.

London docks in the eighteenth century

The 1980s saw a renewed interest in both the US and the UK, and today's modern British IPAs are a revival of the Burton-on-Trent style.

TRY: *FULLER'S IPA, SAMUEL SMITH INDIA ALE, MEANTIME INDIA PALE ALE, BROOKLYN EAST IPA, THORNBRIDGE JAIPUR INDIA PALE ALE*

TRADITIONAL PORTERS AND STOUTS

Porters and stouts predate IPAs by at least a century. They are dark ales with a robust, roasty character whose name probably originates from the style's early popularity among British proletariat dockworkers. Stout is a spinoff style of porter, originally described as a "stout porter," indicating a stronger, darker beer than the everyday porter.

Porters and stouts range from dark brown to black in color, a result of heavily roasted malts in the mash. Historically, porters were probably slightly acrid and smoky due to unevenly roasted malts. Today, many substyles of porters and stouts exist, including Baltic porters, Irish dry stouts, and imperial stouts.

The Irish dry stout, synonymous with Guinness, is probably the most widely recognized subgenre of stout in the world. Despite its dark, almost black color, the beer is highly refreshing and easy drinking, with a silky mouthfeel and a modest 4 percent ABV. Other variations include creamy oatmeal stouts, oyster stouts brewed with calcium-rich oyster shells, and milk stouts made with sweet lactose sugar.

Imperial stouts are rich, robust stouts scaled up to around 10 percent ABV. Legend dictates they were originally brewed and shipped to the Russian and Baltic states, but, as with IPA, that history is questionable. They continue to be a popular style, though modern iterations are far removed from the original. Today, many are aged in wooden barrels for a doubly concentrated flavor.

Traditional stouts, highly refreshing and easy drinking

Baltic porters are the oddballs of the porter-stout family. They originated as regular British porters, but as cold lager fermentation became popular during the nineteenth century, brewers in the Baltic states began fermenting their porters with lager rather than ale yeast. The shift resulted in a hybrid style that's technically a lager, but with many characteristics of an ale. Today, Baltic porters are considered high-alcohol, cold-fermented beers like imperial stouts.

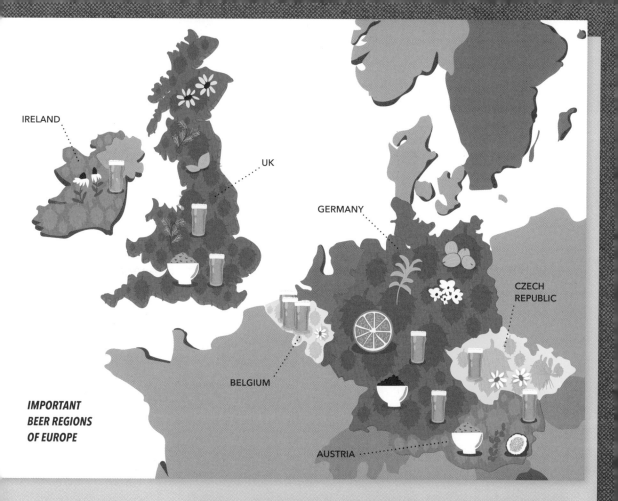

IRELAND

UK

GERMANY

CZECH
REPUBLIC

BELGIUM

**IMPORTANT
BEER REGIONS
OF EUROPE**

AUSTRIA

*TRY: GUINNESS DRAUGHT,
SAMUEL SMITH OATMEAL
STOUT, BROWAR WITNICA S.A.
BLACK BOSS PORTER, FULLER'S
LONDON PORTER, DE DOLLE
SPECIAL EXTRA EXPORT STOUT*

Fuller's London Porter
and Guinness

SAISONS AND FARMHOUSE ALES

Belgium has one of the richest brewing traditions in the world. Different styles define different regions, and some of the most distinctive are the saison and farmhouse ales of Wallonia in southern Belgium. Wallonia borders the Nord and Pas-de-Calais regions of France, which also share the rich history of agricultural beer with their bière de garde, an important contribution to the world of beer styles. Saison and bière de garde are the pinnacle of farmhouse brews.

Saison means "season" in French and refers to beers brewed throughout the winter and spring for consumption in summer when the temperatures would become too hot for carefully controlled fermentation. Saisons were brewed with added preservatives for long-term storage—typically an abundance of hops or adjuncts like honey or sugar to boost their alcohol. The former was typical of Wallonia and the Hainaut province, while the latter became known as the bière de garde ("provisional beer" or "beer for keeping") of France.

Nearly every farmhouse had its own recipe, so it's hard to pin saison to a single style or even a set of specific characteristics. Since these ales were made by farmers rather than professionally trained brewers, early saisons were probably idiosyncratic ales that reflected the whims and resources of the farm. Indeed, saisons often incorporated many farms' ingredients not commonly found in German or British industrial breweries—unmalted grains like raw wheat and spelt, for instance, or adjuncts like honey and beet sugar. In addition to hops, early saisons included other bittering agents like dandelions and herbs.

path to become a more malt-driven ale. The classic bière de garde is amber in color and about 7 to 8 percent ABV. Rarely is it hoppy or dry.

Other farmhouse ales include grisettes and bière du pays. Grisettes are usually lower in alcohol and lighter in body than saisons. And there is some debate over the name: grisette's primary consumers were Hainaut miners who would return from the mines covered in gray dust (*gris* is gray in French). Bière du pays simply means "country beer," but it's sometimes called a table beer. Bières du pays are low-alcohol, light, and crisp beers meant for everyday sustenance.

TRY: **SAISON DUPONT, BLAUGIES SAISON D'EPEAUTRE, FANTÔME SAISON, LA BAVAISIENNE AMBRÉE, DUPONT LA BIÈRE DE BELOEIL**

Fantôme Brewery in Belgium produces farmhouse-style ales

Modern saisons are more uniform, but the style continues to defy easy categorization. Instead, it's best thought of as an umbrella category that encompasses a variety of beers. A few are dark and full-bodied, but most are light in color, fruity, dry, and exceptionally effervescent. Many saisons are bottle-conditioned and some are exceptionally hoppy.

The modern gold standard is Saison Dupont. It's golden in color with a thick, white head of vigorous carbonation. Aromas are citrusy, earthy, and funky, with an undercurrent of grassy hops and yeast esters. It has a creamy mouthfeel that finishes bone dry, almost tart. I reckon it's one of the best beers in the world.

French bière de garde may have started out very much like saison, but diverged along its historic

TRAPPIST ALES

The history of monastic brewing in Europe dates back many centuries to at least the Middle Ages, when monasteries from different religious orders brewed beer for consumption within and outside their walls.

For monks, beer provided nourishment, both spiritually and physically, as well as a steady source of income. Some of the original monastic breweries survive today and several have been added in the past decade. The most common are Trappist breweries of the Cistercian Order with eleven monasteries making beer throughout Europe and the US. More than half are in Belgium.

There is no one Trappist beer style, however, because each monastery has its own proprietary yeast strains and idiosyncratic brewing methods, characteristics can vary immensely between breweries. Instead, Trappist ales comprise a variety of styles shared among only some of their ranks.

DUBBELS AND TRIPELS

The most common are dubbels and tripels, which correspond to increasingly strong beers. Others use numbers like 6, 8, and 10 to denote different beers of varying strength (the numbers ostensibly refer to alcohol percentages but aren't exact). Other Trappist styles are unique; Brasserie d'Orval, for instance, located at the Abbaye Notre-Dame d'Orval, brews two unique saison-like amber ales that are unlike any other Trappist ales. Orval is a bottle-conditioned ale fermented with Brettanomyces, whereas Petite Orval is a half-strength version sold only at a café near the monastery.

Trappist beer gives physical, spiritual, and financial sustenance to Monks

Dubbels and tripels are the most common Trappist beers. Dubbels tend to be amber to dark brown in color with a heavy caramelized malt flavor. Most are brewed with Belgian candi sugar, which lightens the beer's body while boosting the alcohol content. They're rich, often fruity, and range from 6 to 9 percent ABV. Because each monastery uses its own yeast strain, dubbels vary from mildly spicy to strong notes of coriander and black pepper.

SCRATCH AND SNIFF! *Tripels can be spicy and redolent of clove*

Belgian monks in their beer cellar

Tripels vary significantly from dubbels. They're higher in alcohol, but lighter in color, with a pale, rich, straw-colored hue a shade or two darker than pilsner. They're often brewed with added sugars, which lighten the body and boost the ABV. Most are 8 to 10 percent ABV and are redolent of pear, apricot, honey, clove, and banana. Some contain spices, but most get their spicy nose from the house yeast strain.

QUADS

Many trappist breweries make a version of a dark, strong ale that's usually above 10 percent ABV with complex flavors of red and black dried fruit and aromas of earthy spices. These viscous, chewy, and full-bodied beers are sometimes called Quads or Quadrupels, but that name is mainly popular with secular breweries in the US. Many are bottle-conditioned with added yeast and sugar, which re-ferments the beer right in the bottle for added depth and complexity.

ABBEY BEERS

Adding even more confusion to the mix are so-called Abbey beers. These are beers brewed in the style of Trappist ales, but not by an actual Trappist monastery itself. They can be made by other non-Trappist monastic breweries, commercial breweries, or breweries contracted by an existing monastery.

TRY: ORVAL, WESTVLETEREN 12, CHIMAY BLUE, WESTMALLE TRIPEL, TRAPPISTES ROCHEFORT 10

LAMBIC

Lambic is one of the most revered beer styles in the world. It hails from the Flemish region of Pajottenland near the city of Brussels. At its most basic, it's a sour wheat ale fermented with native yeast. Tannic, acidic, and funky, it often tastes more like a fine wine than a beer. But many peculiar components and processes go into its production.

First, it's brewed with aged rather than fresh hops. These act more as a preservative than a bittering agent. Second, it's made with a piece of brewing equipment called a *koelschip* (or coolship). This cools the hot wort (unfermented beer) overnight. The brewery's windows or roof vents are left open so that wild microflora and yeast can inoculate the beer. These yeast and bacteria will eventually be the sole source of the beer's primary fermentation.

Once the wort is chilled, the liquid is transferred to wooden casks where it ferments for many months and up to several years. The result is tart and highly acidic, with aromas of barnyard funk, lemon, vinegar, and sharp cider.

GUEUZE

With such strong flavors, most lambic needs to be blended with beer of various ages to become palatable. This mix of young and old lambic is called gueuze, and it's the result of masterful blending. In fact, many gueuze blending houses, or "gueuzerie," don't brew beer—they source lambic from producers to make blends of their own.

LEFT A coolship allows for spontaneous fermentation

FRUIT LAMBIC

Fruit lambic is lambic that's been aged on fruit juice, crushed fruit, or whole fruits. The most common example is kriek, made with sour cherries. Others include pêche (peach), framboise (raspberry), and cassis (black currant). Fruit imparts aromas and sweetness that balances pure lambic's acidic flavors.

*TRY: **DE CAM OUDE LAMBIEK, BOON OUDE GEUZE MARIAGE PARFAIT, DRIE FONTEINEN OUDE GEUZE, CANTILLON CLASSIC GUEUZE, HANSSENS OUDE KRIEK***

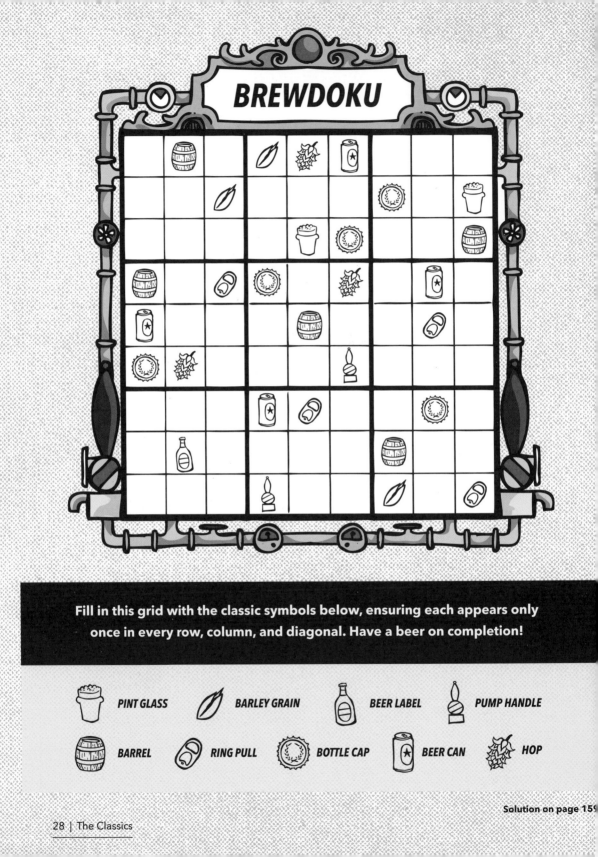

BREWDOKU

Fill in this grid with the classic symbols below, ensuring each appears only once in every row, column, and diagonal. Have a beer on completion!

PINT GLASS   BARLEY GRAIN   BEER LABEL   PUMP HANDLE

BARREL   RING PULL   BOTTLE CAP   BEER CAN   HOP

Solution on page 159

STRONG ALES

Europe and the British Isles have a long history of brewing strong, dark ales for consumption during the cold winter months. These beers go by various names, including winter warmers, barleywines, Belgian strong ales, old ales, and stock ales. Stylistically, most of these beers are distinct, but they have more similarities than differences.

BARLEYWINE

Barleywine is perhaps the most well known example of strong ale. Barleywines are boozy and sweet, with intense flavors of toffee and dark-brown sugar. The style originated in mid-nineteenth-century England, with Bass producing the first commercial example. It was a boozy, sweet ale sold in the wintertime and meant to mimic the flavors and mouthfeel of fortified wines (hence the marketing term "barleywine").

SCRATCH AND SNIFF! Barleywines have sweet aromas of dried fruit

They're nearly indistinguishable from old ales and stock ales, though some argue there are unique, if extremely subtle, differences. Barleywines age beautifully, developing sherry-like aromas of toffee, dried fruit, and caramel. Most modern versions are well over 10 percent ABV.

BELGIAN STRONG ALES

Belgian strong ales are another popular style of boozy ale. They vary from pale to dark brown in color and are distinguished from barleywines by their lavishly fruity yeast aromas. Many are like Trappist tripels or quads, the distinguishing factor being that Belgian strong ales aren't brewed in monasteries.

TRY: DE DOLLE STILLE NACHT, FULLER'S 1845, DE STRUISE PANNEPOT, J.W. LEES HARVEST ALE, ALESMITH OLD NUMBSKULL

RAUCHBIERS—SMOKY GERMAN LAGERS

When it comes to the historic beers of Bamberg, Germany, smoke is an integral flavor. Rauchbiers, as they're called (*rauch* means smoke in German), are one of the most distinctive—and divisive—beer styles in the world.

To some, they taste rich and roasty, like a drinkable smoked meat or a liquid cigar. Others find them acrid and harsh with an aftertaste akin to an ashtray. Many compare their smoky flavor to single-malt Islay Scotch, made from peat-smoked malts.

Many compare their smoky flavor to single-malt Islay Scotch, made from peat-smoked malts.

Smoked beer has more to do with ancient malting techniques imbuing smoke to the grains. Historically, nearly all beers were at least somewhat smoky—practically any grain used for making beer was dried over open fires or via kilns. Grain processed in this way would undoubtedly pick up smoked flavor. But as technology advanced, malts were sprouted under more controlled conditions, allowing brewers to use both smoke-free malts and lighter grains. Despite such advances, the brewers of Bamberg embraced the smoke.

The most common base for a rauchbier is German Märzen—the original Aecht Schlenkerla Rauchbier—an amber-hued 5 percent ABV lager. The brewery also makes smoked versions of hellesbier, bock, and hefeweizen, while others have experimented with smoked stouts, porters, and even pilsners. The latter are typically brewed with smaller percentages of smoked malt, making them palatable

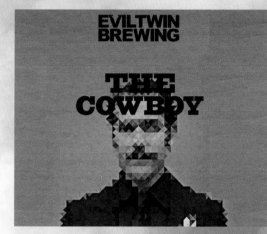

The Cowboy, a smoked beer by Evil Twin Brewing

to drinkers usually turned off by traditional rauchbiers. Rauchbiers age beautifully, their smoke flavors mellowing over time.

TRY: *AECHT SCHLENKERLA RAUCHBIER MÄRZEN, ALASKAN SMOKED PORTER, MIKKELLER BEER GEEK BACON, GÄNSTALLER BRÄU AFFUMICATOR, EVIL TWIN THE COWBOY*

NEW WORLD

In this chapter, we'll explore in some detail American craft beers, and discover why they're "hoppier" than their British counterparts.

IPA might have originated centuries ago in the UK, but today it is inextricably linked to modern American craft beer. These New World hop bombs are far removed from the traditional British style. American IPAs are aggressively bitter, often high in alcohol, and heady with pungent hop aromas.

They've also inspired the "hopification" movement that has transformed many other traditional beer styles like brown ales and pilsners into hop monsters. Today, nearly any beer labeled "American style" all but guarantees a nominally hoppy one, regardless of what tradition dictates of the style.

Zero 2 Sixty is a sour beer from Two Roads Brewing Company in Connecticut, U.S.

AMERICAN IPA

American IPAs come in many forms—from sessionable low-alcohol varieties to double-digit imperial IPAs—but as a whole, the style is the most popular in craft beer, accounting for nearly 30 percent of all craft sales annually—and still growing. There are now more than a dozen different subgenres with new iterations and regional variations constantly popping up. It's like craft brewers just can't seem to stop themselves from tinkering with and expanding the category.

Compared with many newer types, the first American IPAs were somewhat comparable to their British antecedents. Two of the earliest were Anchor Brewing Co.'s Liberty Ale, first brewed in 1975 in San Francisco, and New Jersey's Ballantine IPA, which dates back much earlier to the late 1800s. Both are moderately boozy with a full-flavored hop presence, a pleasant bitterness, and suggestively aromatic hop notes of grapefruit and pine.

But the real godfather of today's American IPA is Sierra Nevada's Pale Ale with its bright, citrusy, hop-forward flavor. First developed in 1980, it set the stage for nearly all modern American IPAs that followed. Today's American IPAs are decidedly bitter and hoppy. Instead of the

mildly grassy, minty aromas of English IPAs, American versions reek of resin, citrus, and pine. These aromas come from myriad American hop breeds, which are often engineered to maximize their over-the-top aromas.

WEST COAST-STYLE IPA

One of the original subcategories of American IPA is the West Coast–style IPA. Though now made worldwide, it originated in southern California in the 1990s with breweries like AleSmith, Ballast Point, and Stone. West Coast IPA is amped up on all fronts—a more pronounced hop character, a higher alcohol percentage (around 7 percent ABV), and, especially, even more bitterness than other American IPAs—though it's no longer a geographical indication of style, as many breweries in southern California moved on to other styles.

AMERICAN DOUBLE IPA

Closely related, geographically and stylistically, is the American double IPA, which also originated in 1990s southern California. It has an intense hoppiness and an elevated alcohol content (usually between 8 to 10 percent ABV) resulting from extra malts used in the brewing process. Like American and West Coast IPAs, the style is both hoppy and bitter, but with some residual sweetness that makes it easy drinking. Double IPAs are sometimes referred to as imperial IPAs, though there are arguably some distinctions (imperial IPAs can reach well into the double-digit alcohol range).

SCRATCH AND SNIFF! American IPAs contain notes of pine

SESSION IPA

These low-alcohol ales—usually below 5 percent ABV—are relatively new inventions that aim to capture all the flavors of a regular American IPA, but in a smaller, more manageable package. The idea is to "session" them—consume one after another—throughout the day, without getting too sloshed. The style has become a favorite of day-drinkers and the outdoor set who pack them for hikes, fishing trips, and other outdoor activities.

Other American IPA variants include Brett IPA (fermented with Brettanomyces yeast), black IPA (a dark hoppy beer brewed with roasted malts and sometimes called Cascadian dark ale), and Northeast-style IPA (a hazy, low-bitterness style often sold in 16 oz aluminum cans). There's even the IPL—India pale lager—which is structured like an IPA, but fermented at lower temperatures for several weeks with a clean, lagering yeast strain.

TRY: SIERRA NEVADA TORPEDO, MAINE BEER LUNCH, HALF ACRE GONEAWAY

AMERICAN INGENUITY

Genesee Brewing Company beer storage tanks

CALIFORNIA COMMON

California common is another American invention. In some regards it's the opposite of cream ale in that it uses a strain of lager yeast that ferments at warmer ale temperatures rather than a typically frigid one. The style evolved during the California gold rush when brewers who made cold-fermented lagers in cold caves began fermenting in California's warm climes. As they headed west, brewers took along only lagering yeast, which had to be morphed into something that could work in California's balmy climate. This warm-fermented lager became known as the "common" beer of nineteenth-century California. It was also the era of the steam engine and the style was often dubbed steam beer. Several examples are still brewed today, most notably Anchor Steam in San Francisco.

CREAM ALE

Cream ale, along with California common (or steam beer), is one of only two indigenous beer styles attributable to American brewers. It contains no cream or dairy at all, but is a hybrid of classic German lagers and American ales. Cream ales are technically fermented with ale yeast, but at much lower temperatures than traditional ales—much closer to bottom-fermenting lager temperatures in fact. Some cream ales even use both ale and lager yeast during fermentation. The result is a clean, smooth ale free of the fruity esters that are typical of traditional ales.

TRY: ANCHOR STEAM, GENESEE CREAM ALE, SIXPOINT SWEET ACTION

HOPPED-UP CLASSICS

Brown ales are often considered an unwelcome holdover of the 1990s American "microbrewery" phenomenon—boring beers from an era when "color" beers reigned (i.e., blonde ale, red ale, brown ale, etc.). But brown ale is an easily enjoyable craft brew for beginners.

American brown ales are constantly subjected to refinement and experimentation, as American brewers find new ways to make them exciting again. Sometimes that means adding a bevy of hops to make for an aromatic, heady brew, or fermenting with an unusual yeast. Because of their mild, nutty flavors, many are great for pairing with food, especially with Maillard-enriched dishes like roasted root vegetables and grilled chicken.

Another traditional style gilded by the American hop is the porter. American porters are more aggressively roasty, ruthlessly bitter, and often noticeably hoppy. Same goes for American wheat ales. The witbiers and hefeweizens of Belgium and Germany are well-balanced, softly aromatic beers redolent of clove, banana, coriander, and orange peel. Their American counterparts are often more reminiscent of IPA brewed with wheat.

Today, many American brewers make hoppy pilsners as summer seasonals and everyday shift beers. The style is considerably different from India pale lagers, as the base beer is a traditional pilsner that's dry-hopped after the boil with aromatic American and German hops.

TRY: **SURLY BENDER, GREAT LAKES EDMUND FITZGERALD, ALLAGASH WHITE, VICTORY PRIMA PILS**

AMERICAN SOUR ALES

If any one category is threatening IPA's reign as America's most popular beer style, it's sour ales. But, despite its perception of a single, codified thing, sours is a maddeningly overbroad category encompassing many disparate styles that have little in common with one another.

Why make a sour beer in the first place? Before pasteurization, nearly every beer was probably touched with a hint of sourness—usually unintentionally and usually the result of a poor understanding of microbiology. But since the late nineteenth century, most brewers have tried—with great success—to keep souring microbes out of their beer.

Off-Color's Troublesome gose is brewed with *Lactobacillus*

Today, sour-on-purpose beer is an increasingly popular category, especially in the US and in Europe, with the rise of many new sour-only breweries. It includes beer influenced by the traditional lambics and Flanders reds of Belgium, and Berliner weisses and goses of Germany.

So-called sours can be thought of as two distinct groups: simple sours and aged sours. Simple sours are based on the German method of making quick-fermented ales spiked with the bacteria *Lactobacillus* and sometimes the yeast strain Brettanomyces. They include Berliner weisse and gose, two tart, low-alcohol beers that date back centuries. Aged sours, on the other hand, originated in Belgium with lambics, oud bruins, Flanders reds, and some saisons. They are proper barrel-aged beers that undergo a much longer, more complex fermentation process that lasts many months and sometimes even years.

Sour Bikini is a light-bodied, well-balanced sour pale ale

SIMPLE SOURS

Two of the most popular American simple sours are the Berliner-style weisse and the American gose. As the name implies, Berliner weisse is a tart, refreshing *weisse* (wheat) ale that originated in Berlin several centuries ago. It was once the most popular style in its namesake city, but is nearly obsolete in modern-day Berlin. It's traditionally served in a wide, shallow glass with a squirt of fruit or herb *schuss* (syrup). Gose (pronounced *goes-uh*) is a similar simple German sour ale native to Leipzig. It's a peculiar beer that historically incorporated salt and coriander.

Over the past decade, American brewers have adulterated and transmuted these two tart ales into a form that's all their own. Very few American Berliner-style weisse are served with a shot of sweetening syrup. Instead, they have fruits and juices incorporated into the beer pre-packaging.

The same goes for American goses—many contain far more salt than traditional ones, while others have a pronounced hop presence, something you'd never find in Germany. And, like American Berliner-style weisse, many goses incorporate fruit and herbs (often citrus and mint) right into the beer itself. That doesn't necessarily make any of these bad beers; they're just very different from the historic ales of Germany.

The American hoppy sour ale is a hybrid style somewhere between American IPA and German simple sour. Amped up with massive dry hopping, these beers have huge aromas of tropical and citrus fruit that complement the beer's tartness.

*TRY: **J. WAKEFIELD DRAGONFRUIT PASSIONFRUIT BERLINER WEISSE, OFF COLOR TROUBLESOME, EVIL TWIN SOUR BIKINI***

AGED SOURS

Americans are dabbling with more complex sour ales, too. In fact, coolships like those used in Belgian lambic production are increasingly common fixtures in many American breweries. The beers are made in the same way as lambics—that is, they are cooled in a coolship, exposed to ambient air overnight, and racked into wooden casks and barrels for long fermentation. However, American-made spontaneous ales are never labeled lambic or gueuze, since those designations are reserved for only Belgian brewers. Instead, they're referred to simply as spontaneous ales or sometimes "Méthode Gueuze," a designation like *méthode champenoise.*

More common still are mixed fermentation ales. The main distinction between American spontaneous ales and mixed fermentation ales (sometimes called "wild ales") is that the latter contain pitched yeast strains and added bacteria cultures. This means the brewer intentionally added yeast and bacteria to the beer during fermentation rather than relying solely on ambient air microbes. Though processes vary from brewery to brewery, the common thread is a base beer fermented over a long period with several different yeast strains and bacteria. The beer is then aged in oak barrels, foeders, or other vessels for many months.

Most mixed fermentation ales are bottle-conditioned with yet another dose of yeast. Stylistically, these are more like Belgian saisons than lambic in that they are tart, dry, and effervescent, with myriad aromas from the various yeast esters and barrel aging.

TRY: JESTER KING SPON, HOLY MOUNTAIN WITCHFINDER

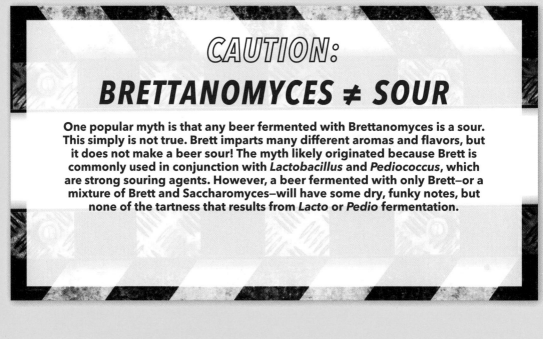

CAUTION:
BRETTANOMYCES ≠ SOUR

One popular myth is that any beer fermented with Brettanomyces is a sour. This simply is not true. Brett imparts many different aromas and flavors, but it does not make a beer sour! The myth likely originated because Brett is commonly used in conjunction with *Lactobacillus* and *Pediococcus*, which are strong souring agents. However, a beer fermented with only Brett—or a mixture of Brett and Saccharomyces—will have some dry, funky notes, but none of the tartness that results from *Lacto* or *Pedio* fermentation.

BEER MENU

When visiting your local craft beer store, here is the type of thing you'd expect to find on the menu. This one's adapted from a menu by Tørst, NYC.

BEER NAME
The name of the particular beer or brand

BREWERY
The name of the brewery that produces the beer

STYLE
The style of the beer, whether it's an IPA, brown ale, saison, pilsner, lambic, etc

NC1 APPALACHIAN FARMHOUSE
Transmitter Brewing
SAISON/FARMHOUSE ALE • LONG ISLAND CITY, NY • 6.8% ABV • 20 IBU
A collaboration between New York's Transmitter and Asheville's Burial Beer Co. A farmhouse ale with winter white wheat, cracked raw wheat, wildflower honey, and foraged sumac, all from North Carolina.

XX-BITTER
Brouwerij De Ranke
IPA–BELGIAN • DOTTIGNIES, HAINAUT, BELGIUM
This "extra extra bitter" is famous for its very bitter and strong flavor, made with pale pilsner malt and loads of Brewers Gold and Hallertau hop flowers.

TOASTED MARSHMALLOW IPA
Decadent Ales
IPA–AMERICAN • MAMARONECK, NY • 7% ABV
Our IPA recipe with toasted marshmallows is brewed with Madagascar vanilla beans and a variety of candied, turbinado, and coconut sugars to create the mellow sweetness of a campfire-toasted marshmallow.

BEERBRUGNA
LoverBeer
SOUR ALE • MARENTINO, TO, ITALY • 6.2% ABV
Inoculated by wild yeasts and bacteria, we add small, dark, and sweet Damaschine plums to restart fermentation. The beer is then matured in oak barrels for twelve months.

CAFFÉ CORRETTO
Carton Brewing Company
CREAM ALE • ATLANTIC HIGHLANDS, NJ • 12% ABV • 20 IBU
Caffé Corretto is our golden imperial coffee cream ale, regular coffee, finished with fennel, licorice, and anise. It takes a lesson from our Italian friends by running a touch of anise's bitter-to-sweet path alongside coffee's.

LOCATION BREWED
Where the beer comes from, which is increasingly important as interest in local beer and other specialty food products swells

ABV
Alcohol by Volume—since beer ranges from roughly 2–15 percent ABV, this number lets drinkers know what they're in for

IBU
International Bitterness Unit, a measure of bitterness that is sometimes given on menus

DESCRIPTION
The bar's or brewery's notes on the particular beer; can include things like added ingredients, brewing techniques, history, or even just tasting notes

IMPERIAL STOUTS AND BOURBON BARREL-AGED BEER

Barrel-aged American imperial stouts is a style so popular that many breweries hold entire festivals dedicated to their special imperial stout releases (e.g., 3 Floyds Dark Lord Day or Cigar City's Hunahpu's Day).

Cigar City Hunahpu's Day

Such sweeping acclaim raises the question: Are the beers really that good? Well, yes and no. Imperial stouts are easy to love. They contain familiar childhood flavors that are effortlessly identifiable—namely chocolate, coffee, and vanilla (though most contain none of these actual ingredients). That makes them extremely popular with nearly anyone who enjoys these basic tastes (most of us!).

Imperial stouts originated in late-eighteenth-century England where strong stouts and porters were brewed and shipped to Russia and the Baltic states (they're sometimes called Russian imperial stouts). It's impossible to know exactly what those early beers tasted like, but they were likely less boozy and a little smokier than today's chocolaty alcohol bombs. In addition to chocolate, coffee, and vanilla, American imperial stouts contain sharp, bitter flavors and residual sweetness that ranges from harmonizing to cloying. That makes them extremely popular with nearly anyone who enjoys these basic tastes (most of us!). But often the beer is overwrought and one-note.

One thing many imperial stouts have in common is the variant release. These are serialized collections with a common base beer that's been gussied up with different adjuncts like actual chocolate, actual coffee, roasted chili peppers, or maple syrup. The most widely available is Goose Island's Bourbon County Brand Stout and its variants, which rotate each year.

As with their nonstop showering of hops, American brewers can't help but put nearly any style of beer into a used bourbon barrel. Bourbon barrel–aged IPA? Check. Bourbon barrel–aged brown ale? Check. Bourbon barrel–aged Berliner weisse, saison, and pilsner? Check, check, check. Most beer doesn't improve in the barrel, but some do. The best contenders are high-alcohol styles like

imperial porter, barleywine, and Belgian-style strong ales. Darker beer does better than lighter beer, but not as a fixed rule. In fact, one of the best bourbon barrel–aged beers I've had was a golden-hued Belgian tripel.

TRY: ALESMITH SPEEDWAY STOUT, BELL'S BLACK NOTE STOUT, DIEU DU CIEL, PÉCHÉ MORTEL, ALLAGASH CURIEUX, HAIR OF THE DOG ADAM FROM THE WOOD, BREWDOG BOURBON BABY

Hair of the Dog's Adam has notes of chocolate, leather, and smoke

FOOD BEER

Beginning with the earliest stouts and porters, there have almost always been beers that tasted like coffee. It's simply the result of flavors from dark-roasted malts, which impart bitter, roasty flavors we associate with similarly dark-roasted coffee beans. But coffee beer? Adding actual coffee to your beer? That is something relatively new.

One of the earliest examples was from New Glarus Brewing in Wisconsin, which in the mid-1990s added coffee to its stout. There are now coffee IPAs, coffee lagers, coffee saisons, even coffee sours. The best coffee beers tend to be the classics like stouts, porters, and brown ales.

TRY: ALASKAN HERITAGE COFFEE BROWN

Some brewers pack an entire dish into their brews. Beers like French toast brown ales, taco IPAs, and donut stouts are all the rage among some beer fans. The best evoke fond food memories without being over-the-top with too many flavors.

TRY: FUNKY BUDDHA FRENCH TOAST DOUBLE BROWN ALE

Herbal ales are an increasingly common style. Some hops themselves are reminiscent of herbs like basil, mint, and sage. Brewers have taken to doubling down on these aromas by adding fresh herbs right into the beer.

TRY: LINDEMANS+MIKKELLER SPONTANBASIL LAMBIC

Traditional lambics have been infused with cherries, berries, and other fruit for centuries. Lately, the most popular fruit beer is the citrus IPA. The style started with San Diego's Ballast Point Brewing's Grapefruit Sculpin IPA. The idea was to amplify the beer's inherent hop flavors, which make it burst with citrus and tropical fruit aromas. Now the whole citrus trick is ubiquitous and everyone is on board.

TRY: EVIL TWIN FEMME FATALE YUZU PALE ALE

Looking for a fun way to add more vegetables into your diet? Try a vegetable beer. Pumpkin ales were a staple of early-American colonists who used whatever fermentable sugars were available to make beer. Today, the pumpkin beer craze thrives, but many contain no pumpkin at all, just pumpkin pie spices of ginger, nutmeg, and allspice. Some of the more exciting vegetable beers include root vegetables like beets and carrots.

TRY: FONTA FLORA BEETS, RHYMES AND LIFE

Mongozo Banana is a Belgian white fruit beer

BEER GRUB

You may be surprised at the different types of food that have been added to some beers . . .

COFFEE

CHERRY

BEET

MINT

LEMON

SAGE

CARROT

TANGERINE ORANGE

GINGER

BERRIES

AMERICAN
BARLEYWINE

Barleywines are among the richest, most complex beers in the world. They're all about strength, intricacy, and depth, with a huge emphasis on chewy malts and intense, burly hop aromas.

The style originated in nineteenth-century Britain with Bass's Barley Wine marketed as a competitor to fortified wines like sherry and port. Like those beverages, barleywine is syrupy and thick, with an intriguing nose of complex, oxidative aromas; they are the original extreme beers.

SCRATCH AND SNIFF! American barleywines can have grapefruit aromas

Barleywines are lighter in color than imperial stouts, with a rich, tawny copper to dark reddish-brown hue. They're full-bodied, strong, and sweet, but balanced by intricate fruit flavors and a bitter backbone. American barleywines are like British versions on steroids. Most are at least 9 percent ABV or more. The hops are amped up with bouquets of citrus and pine over an underlay of vinous, toasty malt. Unfortunately, the style often gets overlooked in favor of imperial stouts, which are similar in body and brashness, but are arguably less flavorful, less complex, and less nuanced than barleywine.

The first American barleywine was Anchor's Old Foghorn. Today, it seems very much in the style of its English predecessor, but with one very American twist—Cascade hops. These give it a resinous, grapefruit-like aroma not found in the original English style. Old Foghorn was first brewed in 1975 and revived an interest in barleywine not only in the US, but also in the UK, where the style had all but vanished. Ten years later, Sierra Nevada

introduced its Bigfoot Barleywine, which upped the game even further with thrillingly complex hop aromas and sherry-like flavors. In the thirty-plus years since then, American brewers have continued to one-up one another, pushing the barleywine envelope further and further.

Today, like many imperial stouts, barleywines are often aged in oak casks or bourbon barrels, which round out sharp flavors and dull the sting of booze.

*TRY: **ANCHOR OLD FOGHORN, SIERRA NEVADA BIGFOOT BARLEYWINE, REVOLUTION STRAIGHT JACKET BARLEYWINE, GOOSE ISLAND BOURBON COUNTY BARLEYWINE, HAIR OF THE DOG FRED***

HOP ON!

Hops are one of the key ingredients in beer. They are bittering agents, responsible for many of the aromas, flavors, and smells we associate with it. They also act as preservatives, making beer shelf stable and free from microbiological spoilage.

Hop cones are the female flowers of the *Humulus lupulus* plant, a wildly growing bine belonging to the *Cannabaceae* family, which also includes hemp and marijuana. They're native to several northern hemisphere areas, including North America, Europe, Western Asia, and China, where they have been used for millennia for their sedative and soporific medicinal qualities.

The plants grow comfortably in latitudes of roughly 30 to 50 degrees, but thrive at around 45 degrees. Hops are now cultivated in both the Northern and Southern hemispheres, from New Zealand and China to Albania, South Africa, and Canada. For brewing purposes, hops are classified into three categories: aroma, bittering, and dual-purpose, which means they add both bitterness and aroma. Bittering hops are used during the brewing process; they're added directly into the boil kettle and provide the backbone bitterness associated with most beer.

Hop vines are grown on trellises that are 15–20 ft tall

Aroma hops, on the other hand, are added later in the brewing process, either near the end of the boil, at the whirlpool phase, or even during fermentation, which is called dry hopping. Many of the currently popular hops are considered dual-purpose varieties, meaning they can be used for both aroma and bittering—a recent revelation resulting from hop-breeding programs.

Two numbers commonly associated with hops are alpha acid and beta acid percentages. Alpha acids are the principal components in hop cone resin and act as the primary bittering agent in hops when added to boiling wort. Brewers adjust their recipes and formulas based on hop alpha acid content, which is measured in a laboratory and reported as a percentage of the hop's total weight.

Alpha acids generally range from 2 to 18 percent and indicate the level of bittering potential of a hop used during the brewing process. Since alpha acids are only activated at high temperatures—or "isomerized" in organic chemistry jargon—alpha acids in hops added after the boil or during fermentation do not contribute bitterness at all, only aroma.

Beta acids are also dissolved at high temperatures, but unlike alpha acids they do not isomerize. Instead, they pass unchanged into the beer, adding anti-bacterial qualities, but little bitterness. Hops with a roughly 1:1 ratio of alpha to beta acids are highly sought-after aroma hops, while hops with a larger ratio of alpha to beta acids are used primarily for bittering or so-called dual-purpose that is, both bittering and aroma.

Another hop statistic commonly reported is total essential oil, which gives hops their distinctive aromas. The primary essential oils in hops are humulene, caryophyllene, myrcene, and farnesene. Each contributes its own unique character to the hop's overall aroma, but there are also roughly 300 other compounds that may influence aroma, too.

The global hop industry is exploding, thanks largely to beer lovers' insatiable appetites for hoppier brews. The market push now largely favors super alpha varieties—ones with high alpha acid contents—as well as hops with unique aroma characteristics, which are used for complex, aromatic, and beautifully flavored beers like American double IPAs.

UNITED STATES

The primary hop-growing regions of the US are the Yakima Valley of Washington State and the Willamette Valley of Oregon, both in the Pacific Northwest. The hops grown here vary from bitter and dank to heady and highly aromatic, with notes of citrus, tropical fruit, and pine. Other American hop-growing regions include the Panhandle of Idaho and parts of Michigan.

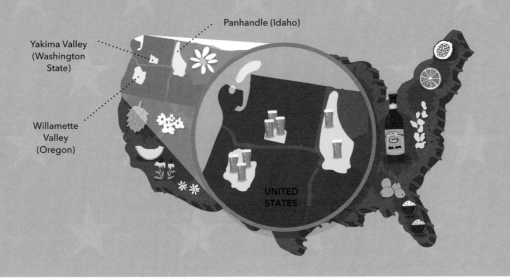

Panhandle (Idaho)

Yakima Valley (Washington State)

Willamette Valley (Oregon)

UNITED STATES

CITRA

Since its release in 2007, Citra has become the hottest hop on the planet. It oozes explosive aromas of citrus—*duh*—but also melon, passion fruit, and gooseberry. Brewers simply can't get enough of it—Citra is quickly becoming one of the highest acreage hops in the US.

SCRATCH AND SNIFF! *Gooseberry is a common aroma in American hops*

FIND IT IN: **OTHER HALF ALL CITRA EVERYTHING, KERN RIVER CITRA DOUBLE IPA**

CASCADE

Cascade is an aroma hop developed by the US Department of Agriculture's hop-breeding program at Oregon State University. It's named after the Cascade Mountains, which traverse its primary growing region—the Willamette and Yakima valleys of the Pacific Northwest. Cascade was first used commercially in the mid-1970s by New Albion Brewing Company in California and later became the signature hop flavor of American pale ales and IPAs.

The hop imparts a ton of different flavors—pine, wildflowers, spice, and citrus—in a single package. The dominant characteristic is grapefruit, but it also brings plenty of floral and evergreen flavors.

*FIND IT IN: **SIERRA NEVADA PALE ALE, ANCHOR LIBERTY ALE***

CENTENNIAL

Centennial is a high-alpha, dual-purpose aroma and bittering hop that's sometimes thought of as Cascade on steroids. It offers bigger floral and grapefruit notes, but a touch less pine than Cascade. It was developed in 1974 at Washington State University, but wasn't released commercially until the 1990s. It is grown throughout the Pacific Northwest.

*FIND IT IN: **FOUNDERS CENTENNIAL IPA, BELL'S TWO HEARTED ALE***

MOSAIC

Another hot new hop is Mosaic. It debuted in 2012 from the Hop Breeding Company and features a complex aroma that hits many different pleasure zones all at once. A cross between American Nugget and Simcoe hops, it's one of the most versatile hops in the world and is often used as the sole hop in single-hop beers.

*FIND IT IN: **PRAIRIE ARTISAN ALES FUNKY GOLD MOSAIC, LOST NATION MOSAIC IPA***

GERMANY AND CZECH REPUBLIC

Each name of the four noble hops of Germany and the Czech Republic refers to a town or region where these hops have been cultivated naturally (not cross-bred) for hundreds of years, developing a high aroma and low bitterness content along the way. These are hops synonymous with Bavarian and Czech pilsners and lagers.

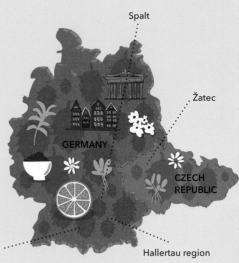

Spalt

Žatec

GERMANY

CZECH REPUBLIC

Tettnang

Hallertau region

HALLERTAU MITTELFRÜH

Hallertau is the original German pilsner hop. It comes from the Hallertau region of Central Bavaria where it was grown for centuries until being largely supplanted by the wilt-resistant Hersbrucker hop in the 1970s. Today, several varieties of Hallertau are still grown in Germany as well as a handful of cultivars in the US, New Zealand, and Australia.

FIND IT IN: BITBURGER PREMIUM PILS, JEVER PILSENER

SAAZ

Saaz are Bohemian hops most commonly associated with Bohemian pilsners, specifically Pilsner Urquell. They're gently aromatic with low bitterness and a spicy, earthy, herbal flavor plus grass and mint aromas. They're named after their place of origin, the Czech town of Žatec (called Saaz in German). In addition to Bohemian pilsners, Saaz is the primary hop found in Stella Artois.

*FIND IT IN: **PILSNER URQUELL, MOONLIGHT REALITY CZECK***

The Czech Republic town of Žatec—where Saaz Bohemian hops come from

TETTNANG

Tettnang comes from a small municipality in the southern Baden-Württemberg region of Germany. Its cultivars are sometimes referred to as Tettnanger, which simply means a person or thing from Tettnang. It's a dual-purpose hop, imparting both mild aroma and bitterness with floral and slightly spicy flavors. Tettnang is used in a wider range of styles than Hallertau and Saaz, including many European pale ales, wheat beers, and saisons.

*FIND IT IN: **HACKER-PSCHORR MÜNCHNER HELL, AYINGER OKTOBER FEST-MÄRZEN***

SPALT

Spalt, or Spalter Spalt, is a Bavarian hop closely related to Saaz. It dates back centuries and is used for its mild aromatic qualities. It's probably the least well known of the German noble hops and is not as widely planted as other noble varieties. More common is Spalt Select, a cross of Spalt and Hallertau Mittelfrüh, developed by Germany's Hops Research Institute.

*FIND IT IN: **DE DOLLE ARABIER, HOFBRAUHAUS BERCHTESGADEN HELL***

UNITED KINGDOM

The UK has a handful of native hops that for centuries have been used for brewing purposes. Many are the parent hops of US-, Australian-, New Zealand-, and South African-bred varieties. The two primary growing areas are Kent and Herefordshire.

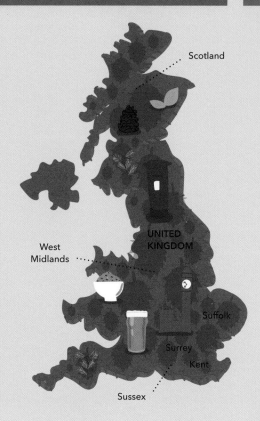

Scotland

West Midlands

UNITED KINGDOM

Suffolk

Surrey

Kent

Sussex

FUGGLE

Fuggle is the classic British aroma hop. It's named after Richard Fuggle, who was responsible for commercializing it from a seedling in the early 1860s. Aromas are grassy, minty, and tea-like against a subtle earthy backdrop. Fuggle is the parent hop to American Centennial, Willamette, and Cascade varieties.

*FIND IT IN: **SAMUEL SMITH OATMEAL STOUT, YOUNG'S SPECIAL LONDON ALE***

GOLDING

Golding is a group of hops with fruity, honey-like flavors and subtle aromas of earth and spice. It is often used in conjunction with Fuggle for bittering and late-hop aromas in British beer. It includes East Kent Golding, which is one of the only hops with an EU Protected Designation of Origin (PDO) status. Golding is one of the parent hops of American Chinooks.

FIND IT IN: *FULLER'S ESB, SAMUEL ADAMS LATITUDE 48 IPA*

A brewer checks the quality of the brew

CHALLENGER

Challenger is a dual-purpose hop first bred at Wye College in Kent as a cross between a Northern Brewer hop and a German variety. It is common in many British beer styles, including stouts and porters, but particularly in extra special/strong bitters (ESBs), brown ales, and other bitters. Its aroma is powerfully spicy with a fruity, floral flavor.

FIND IT IN: *SIERRA NEVADA TUMBLER, DE MOLEN STORM & BLIKSEM*

NORTHERN BREWER

Northern Brewer is grown throughout the world, but it originated in the UK. A cross between Canterbury Golding and a German variety, it's primarily a bittering hop with flavors of pine and mint. Northern Brewer is typical of English pale ales as well as the California common/steam beer style brewed in the US. American-grown Northern Brewer is like a UK-grown version with a distinctive cedar aroma.

FIND IT IN: *ANCHOR STEAM, HAIR OF THE DOG ADAM*

SCRATCH AND SNIFF!

A fresh cedar aroma is found in Northern Brewer

AUSTRALIA

Australia has been cultivating hops down under for more than 200 years and now has nearly a dozen distinct varieties in production. The primary growing regions are located on the island of Tasmania and in the mountainous alpines of Victoria. Most Australian hops are fruity with some floral character but little spice, evergreen, or pine aroma.

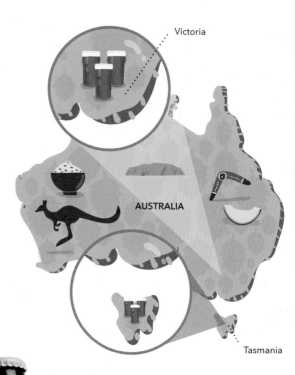

Victoria

AUSTRALIA

Tasmania

GALAXY

Galaxy is by far Australia's most widely recognized specialty hop variety. It's an aromatic hop with intense notes of peach, lime, passion fruit, and melon-like American Citra hops. It's a cross of native high–alpha acid Australian and European cultivars.

FIND IT IN: ANCHORAGE GALAXY WHITE IPA, THE KERNEL INDIA PALE ALE–GALAXY

VIC SECRET

Another quickly rising hop star from Australia is Vic Secret, first introduced commercially in 2011. It's a subtler hop than Galaxy, but shares many of the peach, passion fruit, and citrus flavors. It's often used as a late-addition hop for dry hopping and whirlpooling.

FIND IT IN: CLOUDWATER WINTER RANGE IPA, PIZZA PORT GRAVEYARD'S PALE ALE

NEW ZEALAND

New Zealand's hop-growing region is located at the northern tip of the South Island, with the city of Nelson as its center. New Zealand grows sixteen distinct hop varieties and exports approximately 85 percent of its annual crop to markets around the world. They're increasingly in high demand for their heady tropical fruit aromas, especially among niche European, UK, and US craft brewers.

North Island

Nelson

NEW ZEALAND

South Island

NELSON SAUVIN

By far the most popular and widely used variety of Kiwi hop is Nelson Sauvin. Its name is a mash-up of Nelson and sauvignon blanc, the primary wine grape grown in the region. Nelson Sauvin is aromatic and fruity, imparting a distinctive cool-climate white wine aroma with notes of peach, honeydew, gooseberry, and guava.

FIND IT IN: ALPINE NELSON IPA, TOPPLING GOLIATH ZEELANDER IPA

MOTUEKA

Originally called B Saaz, Motueka is New Zealand's second most popular hop variety. It's a hybrid of the Czech Saaz hops with intense lime, lemon zest, and tropical fruit aromas.

FIND IT IN: SIERRA NEVADA SOUTHERN HEMISPHERE HARVEST IPA, 8 WIRED HOPWIRED

SOUTH AFRICA

South Africa fosters a tiny but emerging hop industry centered on the country's Western Cape province. The hops have generally high alpha acid with intense fruity aromas.

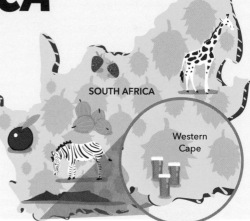

SOUTH AFRICA

Western Cape

SOUTHERN PASSION

Southern Passion has recently eclipsed Southern Brewer as South Africa's most flavorful hop variety. It has intense passion fruit, red berry, and tropical fruit aromas, plus an earthy, spicy quality found in many European noble varieties. Look for it in hop-forward beers like IPAs.

FIND IT IN: CELLARMAKER SOUTHERN PASSION IPA, MODERN TIMES FLOATING WORLD IPA

AFRICAN QUEEN

African Queen is a relatively new South African variety (formerly called J17) with high alpha acid content and dominatingly dank flavors. Aromas include dark berries, peaches, plums, gooseberries, and lemongrass. Like Southern Passion, it's primarily used in hop-forward American-style beers.

FIND IT IN: SOCIETE THE BACHELOR–AFRICAN QUEEN, MODERN TIMES FLOATING WORLD IPA

OTHER HOP-GROWING COUNTRIES

Hops aren't limited to just Western and antipodean countries. In fact, three of the most productive hop-growing countries are ones not commonly associated with beer at all.

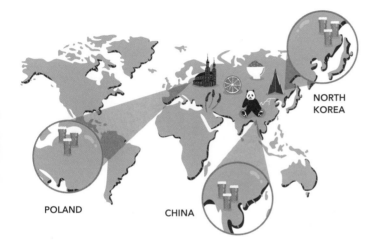

Ethiopia, China, and North Korea all factor prominently into global hop production, with their crops going almost exclusively into international pale lagers. Hops from these regions rarely, if ever, wind up in American or European specialty beer.

GRUIT: THE HOP-FREE BEER

Yes, hops are integral to modern beer's flavors—but that wasn't always the case! One historical beer style called gruit is distinguished because it contains no hops. Instead, bitterness is imparted by a bouquet of herbs and botanicals that commonly includes yarrow, wild rosemary, and bog myrtle.

Up until the Middle Ages, gruits were the norm. But that changed in the sixteenth century with the uprising of political and religious struggles throughout Europe. Many puritanical Christians saw gruit as a witches' brew filled with mind-altering psychedelic and aphrodisiacal elements. They also rejected the Catholic Church's regulation over ale and began using hops for bitterness as a form of protest and rebellion.

Today, gruits are a peculiarity— a niche beverage made by only a handful of specialty brewers.

HOP STATS

Here's a closer look at the elements of some of the most exciting and classic hop varieties.

COUNTRY	HOP NAME	FLAVORS	PURPOSE	ALPHA ACID	BETA ACID	TOTAL OIL (ML/100G)
US	Cascade	Floral, citrus, spicy, grapefruit	Aroma	5.5–9%	6–7.5%	0.8–2.5
US	Centennial	Lemon, floral, citrus	Dual	7–12%	3.5–5.5%	1–3
US	Citra	Grapefruit, melon, lime, gooseberry, passion fruit, lychee	Aroma	11–15%	3–4.5%	1.5–3
US	Mosaic	Blueberry, tangerine, papaya, rose blossom, grassy	Aroma	10.5–14%	3–4.5%	0.8–3
Germany	Hallertau Mittelfrüh	Mild floral, citrus, spicy	Aroma	3–5.5%	3–5%	0.7–1.3
Germany	Tettnang	Spicy, herbal, pepper, black tea	Aroma	3–6%	3–5%	0.5–0.9
Germany	Spalt	Earthy, herbal	Aroma	2.5–5.5%	3–5%	0.5–0.9
Czech Republic	Saaz	Floral, citrus, spicy, herbal, earthy	Aroma	2.5–4.5%	4–6%	0.4–0.8
UK	Fuggle	Earthy, mint, grass, floral	Aroma	3–5.6%	2–3%	0.7–1.4
UK	Golding	Floral, citrus, lemon, grapefruit	Aroma	4–6%	2–3%	0.7–1
UK	Challenger	Floral, herbal, cedar, green tea	Dual	6.5–8.5%	4–4.5%	1–1.7
UK	Northern Brewer	Grassy, mint, pine, herbal	Dual	6–10%	3–5%	1–1.6
Australia	Galaxy	Passion fruit, citrus, fruity	Dual	11.6–16%	5–6.9%	3–5
Australia	Vic Secret	Pineapple, herbal, pine	Aroma	14–17%	6.1–7.8%	2.2–2.8
New Zealand	Nelson Sauvin	Sauvignon blanc, gooseberry, tropical fruit	Dual	12–13%	6–8%	1–1.1
New Zealand	Motueka	Citrus, lime, lemon, tropical fruit	Aroma	6.5–7.5%	5–5.5%	0.7–0.9
South Africa	Southern Passion	Passion fruit, guava, melon, grapefruit	Aroma	8–12%	7–8%	0.9–1.1
South Africa	African Queen	Dank, blueberries, peaches, gooseberries, bubble gum	Aroma	12–17%	6–8%	1.2–.13

HOP *ANATOMY*

The structure of a hop cone

LUPULIN GLANDS

These yellow clusters contain the all-important resins, acids, and essential oils.

BRACTEOLES

These give the hop its structure, and contain the lupulin glands.

BRACT

The hop leaf—this gets discarded after brewing.

STRIG

The footstalk, which contains most of the tannins found in a hop cone.

HOP PROCESSING 101

After harvest, fresh hop cones are spread onto a long, wide conveyor belt and exposed to a constant blast of hot (140°F) air. This slow, steady drying process preserves the hops for use throughout the year until the next harvest. From there, the dried hop leaves are either transformed into pellets or used whole. These are the different forms of hop:

PELLETS

The most common form of post-harvest hop, these small, cylindrical pellets are approximately six millimeters in diameter. They're formed via an automated industrial process. After being dried, whole-leaf hops are pulverized and shredded into dust, which is compacted and then pressed through a die. Because the die creates high temperatures that can diminish the flavor of the hop, the pellets are cut and immediately chilled to around 40°F. From there, they're dropped and sealed into aluminized Mylar foil bags, which protect them from oxygen and other spoilers.

WHOLE CONE

Pelletized hops are easier to store, measure, and use than dried whole cone hops. But some brewers claim the processing destroys or diminishes the hops' flavor and aroma. An alternative is to use whole-cone hops (sometimes called whole-leaf or whole flower hops). These are particularly well suited for dry hopping, as they are easier to remove from the beer after the dry-hopping process is complete. Whole cones may impart fresher aromas than pelletized hops, which can lose essential oils during the pelletization process.

FRESH

Post-harvest, a small percentage of hops is left untouched for use in fresh hop beers. These are made within twenty-four hours of hops being plucked from the fields, a process that captures volatile oils and sticky resins that almost instantly begin fading after harvest. The effect is like using fresh herbs rather than dried in a dish—the flavors become bright, clean, and crisp, with aromas of fresh-cut grass, springtime herbs, and ripe citrus.

Look for fresh hop beers just after the hop harvest has finished—beginning in October in the Northern Hemisphere or April in the Southern Hemisphere. Most are available for only a short time and in limited quantities. Because of their ephemeral nature and delicate flavors, fresh hop beers are best consumed as quickly as possible.

FIVE FRESH HOP BEERS TO TRY:
SIERRA NEVADA HARVEST IPA, FOUNDERS HARVEST ALE, LAGUNITAS BORN YESTERDAY PALE ALE, DESCHUTES CHASIN' FRESHIES, DRIFTWOOD SARTORI HARVEST IPA

RIGHT Workers processing hops in a modern hop farm

HOP QUIZ!

MULTIPLE CHOICE QUESTIONS

1. APART FROM THEIR FOUR PRIMARY ESSENTIAL OILS, HOW MANY OTHER COMPOUNDS IN HOPS MAY INFLUENCE THEIR AROMA?
- A) 200
- B) 300
- C) 500

2. WHEN WAS THE CASCADE VARIETY FIRST USED COMMERCIALLY?
- A) 1920s
- B) 1950s
- C) 1970s

3. WHICH GERMAN HOP VARIETY IS WILT RESISTANT?
- A) HERSBRUCKER
- B) HUDSUCKER
- C) HODCHUCKER

4. THE SAAZ HOP IS FEATURED MOST PROMINENTLY IN WHICH BIG-BRAND BEER?
- A) HEINEKEN
- B) BECKS
- C) STELLA ARTOIS

5. WHICH HOP WAS DEVELOPED AT WASHINGTON STATE UNIVERSITY IN 1974?
- A) MOSAIC
- B) CENTENNIAL
- C) CITRA

6. WHICH HOP CAN BE FOUND IN THE BEER AYINGER OKTOBER FEST-MÄRZEN?
- A) TETTNANG
- B) TETRIS
- C) TRANMERE

7. WHAT'S THE CLASSIC BRITISH AROMA HOP?
- A) WOGGLE
- B) MUGGLE
- C) FUGGLE

8. WHICH HOP WAS FIRST BRED AT WYE COLLEGE, KENT?
- A) CHALLENGER
- B) GOLDING
- C) GALAXY

Have you done your hop homework? To see what you've picked up from this scientifically flavored chapter, pit your wits against these questions . . .

STRAIGHT QUESTIONS

14. HOPS WITH A 1:1 RATIO OF ALPHA TO BETA ACIDS ARE SOUGHT FOR WHICH PARTICULAR QUALITY?

9. WHICH OTHER PLANTS BELONG TO THE CANNABACEAE FAMILY, ALONGSIDE THE PLANT THAT PRODUCES HOP FLOWERS?

15. WHICH ONE OF THE FOLLOWING FLAVORS IS NOT IMPARTED BY THE CASCADE HOP: PINE, WILDFLOWERS, COCOA, SPICE, OR CITRUS?

10. WHAT ARE THE THREE MAJOR CATEGORIES THAT HOP VARIETIES FALL INTO?

16. WHERE IS THE US DEPARTMENT OF AGRICULTURE'S HOP-BREEDING PROGRAM BASED?

Solution on page 159

11. WHAT DOES "ISOMERIZED" MEAN?

12. AT WHICH LATITUDE DO HOPS TEND TO THRIVE MOST ABUNDANTLY?

13. ALPHA ACIDS ARE THE PRINCIPAL COMPONENTS OF WHAT?

DRY HOPPING

Dry hopping is the practice of adding hops to beer after the brewing process—either during the fermentation or conditioning phase—to impart even more heady aroma without added bitterness. Extremely aromatic hops that tickle the fancy of the brewers are often the primary candidates for use in dry hopping.

Dry hopping began with English pale ales, starting in the nineteenth century. The practice was to dump a handful of whole dried hops into the cask before serving, infusing it with extra-fresh hop aroma, and perhaps even disguising a batch of old beer. Today, the practice is synonymous with American craft brewers who have taken it to another level, adding extra hops at nearly every stage and turn of the process.

Instead of dry hopping in the cask, most brewers now do it in the fermentation vessel itself. The cleanest method is with whole-cone hops that are easier to remove from the liquid afterward than hop pellets that break up and suspend in the liquid and can clog and cloud a beer. But many American brewers use hop pellets to dissipate the hop flavors throughout the beer more efficiently. Another technique is to stuff a mesh bag full of whole-cone dried hops and suspend it in the fermentation vessel, a bit like a tea bag.

Some brewers use more high-tech methods for infusing hops. The hopback is a generic device that runs unfermented wort through whole-cone hops, while the HopRocket™ is an increasingly common tool for dispensing more hops at a variety of stages. Others rely on a hop cannon to blast pressurized charges of hop pellets into a holding tank.

The most commonly dry-hopped beers are American IPAs and double IPAs. The additional hops create an expressive and beautifully aromatic beer that's unlike any other in the world.

FIVE DRY HOPPED BEERS TO TRY:
SIERRA NEVADA HOPTIMUM IMPERIAL IPA, TRILLIUM DOUBLE DRY HOPPED FORT POINT PALE ALE, THE VEIL CRUCIAL TAUNT, OMNIPOLLO NEBUCHADNEZZAR IPA, DOGFISH HEAD 90 MINUTE IPA

LEFT Fermentation tanks used for fermenting beer

GRAINS GALORE

These days, hops get all the credit for imparting beer with heady flavors and aromas—and most brewers happily let grains fade into the background. But grains are the real brains behind the beer—the substance responsible for color, mouthfeel, and body, and provides the sugars that yeast produces into alcohol.

Many different types of grain are used to make beer—wheat, spelt, oats, corn, and rice, just to name a few examples—but malted barley is by far the most widely used. In fact, nearly all beers, including wheat beer and those made with corn and rice, use malted barley as the primary fermentable sugar (the only exception being gluten-free beer, which uses sorghum as the primary starch).

What is malted barley? Malting is a process that primes a grain for brewing by activating starches and sugars, which, when mixed with hot water, will ultimately form the base of beer. Nearly any grain can be malted, so "malt" and "barley" are not synonymous terms. Malted wheat is used to make wheat beer and malted rye for rye beer, for example. But in general, when brewers refer to "malt," they usually mean malted barley.

WHY MALT?

What's the point of malting grain in the first place? Raw, unmalted grains contain starches, but they are locked up inside the grain—try steeping unmalted barley in hot water and not much happens. Malting changes this so that the grain readily gives up complex carbohydrates and starches when used in brewing. It's a three-step process that includes steeping, germination, and drying.

Raw grains are first submerged off and on for about two days, during which time they absorb water, increasing their overall moisture content from roughly 10 to 45 percent. The swelled grains then undergo germination, in which protein and carbohydrates break down, opening the starch reserves. This process takes about four days and is facilitated with warm, humid air passing over the grain bed. Then comes the drying phase, which halts germination (if the grain were allowed to continue, it would sprout into a fully realized plant).

The amount of drying depends on how the grain will be used for beer. So-called base malts—the standard golden-colored grains used in most brewing—are kiln-dried at around 190°F for several hours. Specialty malts on the other hand—ones used for more robust flavors and darker beers—are dried at higher temperatures for extended periods of time so that they caramelize and roast.

SCRATCH AND SNIFF! Malts caramelize to produce a sweet aroma

Different grain for brewing beer

MONSTER MASH!

Here are some short definitions of what goes into making a malt mash:

GRAIN BILL
Also called malt bill or mash bill, the grain bill is the list of grains included in the mashing process when hot water is added to malt to extract fermentable sugars. A grain bill almost always includes a high proportion of malted barley and sometimes other grains like rice, corn, and wheat.

MASHING
This is the first step in brewing. Hot water is added to milled malt to extract flavors and sugars. The hot grain and water slurry is allowed to steep and rest at certain temperatures and for exact periods of time in order to activate enzymes in the grain, which convert unfermentable starches to fermentable sugars.

WORT
This is the liquid extracted from the mash. It is sweet and full of sugars, which will eventually ferment the wort into beer, creating alcohol and carbon dioxide along the way.

BACKGROUND A brewery's mash tun copper tanks

MALT MAKES ITS MARK

So how does malted grain influence beer? In nearly every way possible! Malt is the primary culprit for determining a beer's color, body, mouthfeel, and ABV. It also adds flavor and some aroma.

COLOR Unless fruit or some other coloring agent is added to beer, malt is how beer gets its color. Color is directly related to how much and which kinds of malt are used. For example, light beers use light, straw-colored base malts, while dark beers incorporate specialty dark malts. Brown ales use lighter roasted malts; red ales use caramel malts. But note that in darker beers, dark malt is not the *only* malt used, just an important player in the overall grain bill. Also, dark beer does not equal strong beer! Some of the strongest beers in the world are light in color, while some of the lightest are dark.

BODY AND MOUTHFEEL Beer has a sweeping range of textures, from watery and insipid to velvety, thick, and coating. And nearly all of it has to do with sugars—both fermentable and unfermentable—and proteins extracted from the grain bill. Think of body as a general descriptor of the thinness, thickness, or robustness of a beer, while mouthfeel can be used to describe specific physical sensations, such as dryness, astringency, warmth, and carbonation. On a very basic level, full-bodied beers like barleywine are brewed with more malt than light-bodied beers. Light-bodied beers like pilsners use less grain for fewer fermentable sugars.

ALCOHOL Closely linked to body and mouthfeel is ABV. This indicates the total volume of liquid that is made up by alcohol. Alcohol content is determined by the amount of fermentable sugars that the yeast ferment (chew up) and turn into (spit out). High-alcohol beers are typically made with an abundance of fermentable sugars (more grain or added adjuncts), making them boozy with a warming mouthfeel. Low-alcohol beers are the opposite, usually light on the palate, brisk, and refreshing, though there are some exceptions to these generalizations.

BARLEY

Malted barley is by far the grain most often used to make beer. It forms the base for every style, from the lightest pilsner to the darkest imperial stout. Nearly any grain can be malted, but barley is synonymous with this technique.

Malt has a robust husk that doubles as a protectant against damage from rough handling during germination and as a filtration medium in the brewhouse, naturally filtering the wort for a bright, clean liquid for efficient fermentation.

Barley can be classified in many ways. The most common classifications in beer-speak are two-row and six-row. (Others include winter or spring, and malting or feed.) Two-row and six-row refer to the arrangement of the individual grain kernels on a head of barley, and how many are fertile. Two-row barley appears to have only two rows of grain, one along each side of the head, while six-row contains a mutant gene producing six rows of grain along the length of the head.

Brewers use both two- and six-row barley for brewing, but how do these differences translate in the glass? In general, six-row barley has higher protein and more enzymes than two-row, which has a more uniform grain size and higher starch content, making it optimal for grist production when milled in the brewhouse. However, economically, six-row is a superior product for farmers, because the carbohydrate yield is much higher in a single crop. Flavor-wise, brewers prefer two-row because it supposedly creates a malty, full-flavored beer, while some say six-row produces gritty, grainy beer.

Depending on the amount of drying and roasting, malt can be classified into a handful of categories, such as:

BASE MALTS are the everyday brewing malts and include pale malt, pilsner malt, and Vienna malt, as well as several others. They can also include non-barley malts like malted wheat, spelt, and rye. Base malts can be named for their structure (two-row, six-row), the location where they were harvested (Moravia in the Czech Republic), the type of beer they're used in (pilsner malt), or their barley variety (Marris Otter). This leads to a breadth of malt variety for brewers. Base malts make up at least 50 to 100 percent of any beer's grain bill.

BARLEY *TYPES*

The two different types of barley used in brewing beer may look very similar, but they can produce very different flavors.

TWO-ROW

SIX-ROW

Two-row barley creates
a malty, full-flavored beer

Six-row barley purportedly
produces a gritty, grainy beer

CRYSTAL MALTS add color and sweetness to beer and are usually named based on a color scale of light to dark. Lighter crystal malts give sweetness, while darker ones add toffee-ish, burnt caramel flavor and bittersweetness. The extremely light ones are called dextrin malts, which contribute a thick, robust mouthfeel and full body to beer.

ROASTED AND DARK MALTS are dried at high temperatures for a prolonged period, giving a dark color and roasty flavor. There is a wide variety of styles, but the three most common, in order of increasing degree of roast, are chocolate malt, black patent malt, and roast barley. Dark malts give huge flavor, aroma, and color even when used in small quantities. The highest percentage for

dark malts is usually about 10 percent of the overall grain bill.

OTHER MALTS AND ADJUNCTS include malted wheat, spelt, and rye, which take on much smaller supporting roles in the overall grain bill. Adjuncts include corn and rice, common in many North American and Asian beers. (These are covered in detail below.) Adjuncts can also be added along with fermentable sugars like honey, pumpkin, potatoes, and other starchy vegetables.

A brewer checks in on his kettle

GRAIN-FREE AND
GLUTEN-REDUCED BEER

If it isn't made with grain, is it actually beer? That's a question that's been hotly debated for years. But beer made with no-gluten grains like oats and sorghum are the safe option for people with celiac disease.

For a long time, most gluten-free products were pretty vulgar. That was especially true of gluten-free beer. But the landscape has changed over the past several years and some gluten-free options are now downright delicious.

What's the problem with gluten anyway? Those with celiac disease can't easily digest the protein known as gluten, one of the many proteins found in most grains used for brewing. In these folks, gluten causes paralyzing stomach pains and massive sickness, which makes consuming beer, pasta, or bread next to deadly.

The "gluten-sensitive" debate continues to rage. This includes people who haven't been diagnosed with celiac disease, but have some level of discomfort when consuming gluten. For drinkers hoping to reduce their gluten intake or minimize gluten sensitivities, "gluten-reduced" or "crafted to reduce gluten" beers are a godsend.

Gluten-reduced beers are made like other beers, but an enzyme is added during the fermentation stage. This efficient enzyme reduces the gluten content down to fewer than twenty parts per million, below the Codex Alimentarius standard for gluten-free products. But gluten-reduced beers can never be labeled strictly "gluten free," because they're derived from grain-based recipes.

For celiacs, there is no spectrum of gluten—it's either gluten free or it isn't.

TRY: *STONE DELICIOUS IPA, WICKED WEED GLUTEN FREEK, BREWDOG VAGABOND PALE ALE, ALPINE BEER COMPANY EXPONENTIAL HOPPINESS**

*San Diego County's Alpine Brewing adds a gluten-reducing enzyme to most of its beers, making nearly all of them suitable for drinkers seeking to reduce their gluten intake.

BERRY 7.7%	220.- / -	**19**	TO ØL: LIQUID CONFIDENCE IMPY STOUT 12.2%	220.- / -	**25**	ALPHA STATE: NZ IPA 6.5%	180.- / 360.-
CHEE 7.7%	220.- / -	**20**	CÙT CÀ PHÊ BIA (BA PORT) IMP STOUT 11.0%	300.- / -	**26**	BRODIES: HACKNY RED RED IPA 6.1%	170.- / 340.-
RY 7.7%	190.- / -	**21**	TO ØL: GOLIAT IMP STOUT 10.1%	190.- / -	**27**	BRODIES: HOXTON SPECIAL IPA 6.6%	170.- / 340.-
A 5.6%	160.- / 320.-	**22**	GEORGE! IMP STOUT 12.12%	220.- / -	**28**	LOVERBEER: D'UVA BEER SOUR ALE 8.0%	200.- / 400.-
NT 5.0%	160.- / 320.-	**23**	RIS A LA M'ALE FRUIT ALE 6.3%	170.- / 340.-	**29**	TO ØL: MINE IS BIGGER THAN YOURS BARLEY WINE 12.5%	280.-
10.9%	280.-	**24**	ÅRH HVAD! BELGIAN ALE 6.8%	170.- / 340.-	**30**	SCHNEIDER: UNSER AVENTINUS WEIZENBOCK 8.2%	160.- / 320.-

OTHER GRAINS

Although barley is predominantly used in brewing beer, a number of alternative grains are also used.

TURN UP THE WHEAT

Behind barley, wheat is the second most popular grain among traditional and craft brewers. But, unlike barley, it isn't always malted before entering the mash. In fact, many wheat beer styles use raw or unmalted wheat in the grain bill.

The most famous wheat beer styles are the weissbiers of Germany and witbiers of Belgium. (*Weiss* and *wit* mean "white" in their respective languages, but the etymology is derived from the same source as "wheat.") These styles are copied in the US with a noticeable hop presence and often a fruit component like coriander and orange peel (as traditionally used in Belgium).

Wheat lends beer a touch of acidity and a creamy mouthfeel. That acidity makes it perfect for light dishes and thirst-quenching warm weather.

TRY: ALLAGASH WHITE, SCHNEIDER WEISSE ORIGINAL, THE BRUERY WHITE CHOCOLATE

YOU SPELT IT WRONG

Spelt is an ancient variety of wheat that's been used in brewing for millennia. It's largely forgotten today, but is making a comeback as a niche grain in some brewing circles. It often adds an earthy aroma and provides similar flavors and textures as wheat, but with a softly toasty, chewy quality that isn't always present in regular wheat beers. In German, spelt is called dinkel and a dinkelbier—not to be confused with dunkelbier—is an ale made with spelt.

Nowadays, spelt is most frequently used in saisons to provide a rustic grain quality and a fuller, fluffier mouthfeel. It's often used in conjunction with barley, oats, and other grains for complexity and textural depth. It does particularly well with hoppy beers, providing a dry, tight background for the hop aromas to shine.

TRY: HOPWORKS SURVIVAL 7-GRAIN STOUT, BLAUGIES SAISON D'EPEAUTRE

RYES UP

Malted rye adds spiciness, dryness, and a smooth, rounded mouthfeel. It contributes color, too, usually a reddish to light-brown hue. The proportion of rye used in modern beer is typically below 20 percent of the entire malt bill, meaning 80 percent is still made up of malted barley or other grains (wheat is common). Rye is high in protein and causes the mash to become gummy and sticky if used in too high a percentage.

Roggenbier is a historic German rye beer. (*Roggen* is German for rye.) Roggenbiers were nearly extinct after the *Reinheitsgebot* forbade the use of any grain but barley in beer. But over the past few decades, a renewed roggen interest has emerged, and the style is alive and well once again. Modern roggenbiers are brownish to dark red in color, about 5 or 6 percent ABV, and robust and warming with a spicy, rye bread–like flavor.

Some American brewers make roggenbier, but today the most popular form of rye beer is the rye pale ale or rye IPA. (Sometimes cheekily called Rye-P-A.) This hybrid style has all the hoppiness of IPA with a peppery, dry kick from rye. Like roggenbiers, they are reddish to rust in color, with big aromas of bread, pine, and citrus.

Another oddball rye beverage is kvass. This low-alcohol Eastern European drink is made from a slurry of water and leftover dark-grained rye bread that has already been baked and gone stale. It was traditionally used to stretch stale bread further and even purify water as the resulting (low-percentage) alcohol kept microorganisms at bay. Kvass isn't technically a beer, but it received experimental interest among American brewers, such as Goose Island, Jester King, and Fonta Flora.

*TRY: **BÜRGERBRÄU WOLNZACHER ROGGENBIER, FIRESTONE WALKER WOOKEY JACK BLACK RYE IPA***

OATSMOBILE

Did you know that oatmeal has been used in beer for centuries? The most familiar example is creamy oatmeal stouts of the UK. Like rye, oats can gum up the mash, so most brewers prefer to keep them below 10 percent of the overall malt bill. They add a distinctive creamy flavor, full-bodied mouthfeel, and decidedly turbid appearance to beer.

Besides oatmeal stouts, oats are increasingly used in American pale ales and IPAs as a way to boost body and mouthfeel without adding extra booze. In fact, flaked oats are now a primary distinctive ingredient in many New England and Northeast-style IPAs. They are high in beta glucans, which add a soft, elegant edge, and they impart a hazy "juicy" quality that's all the rage today.

*TRY: **SAMUEL SMITH OATMEAL STOUT, TIRED HANDS HOPHANDS***

UNI-CORN

Corn is a dirty word when it comes to beer. The crop is a so-called adjunct, adding cheap fermentable sugar but little taste or body. In fact, beer made with corn is lighter in color, flavor, and mouthfeel than beer made with all malted grain—and often it's used for just those purposes (to make a lighter beer). It is most common in American adjunct lagers like Budweiser, Coors, and Miller High Life, where it may be added in many forms, including grits, flaked corn, or corn syrup.

Corn was originally used in American beer to soften the hard, astringent, grainy character of North American six-row barley. Nineteenth-century brewers substituted the plentiful low-protein corn crop for a percentage of malted barley (around 20 percent) to create a lighter, crisper beer like the German pilsners they were accustomed to in Bavaria.

Today, corn is shedding some of its taboo status. It's long been the traditional grain used in bourbon, which is experiencing a serious revival among cocktail and spirits enthusiasts (including many brewers). And whether ironically or not, some small American beer makers are embracing corn as a no-shame ingredient in brewing, using it in hoppy pilsners and other lagers without fear of backlash from consumers.

*TRY: **MILLER HIGH LIFE, STILLWATER CLASSIQUE***

GLORIOUS *GRAINS*

Here are some of the types of grain that are malted to make beer:

OATS

RYE

BARLEY

RICE

WHEAT

Wheat grain

Rye grain

Oat grain

Barley grain

Rice grain

MR. RICE GUY

Like corn, rice is used as an adjunct to lighten and dry out beer. It's the primary adjunct in Asian-style pale lagers, made throughout Asia and particularly favored in South Korea, Thailand, and Japan. One of the most common is Asahi Super Dry, marked by a pronounced dryness from its high proportion of rice in the mash. The beer set off Japan's so-called Dry Wars of the 1980s when breweries pushed for further lightness of body and crispness of flavor in their beers.

Perhaps it's no surprise that rice has now made its way into American styles, largely as a novelty ingredient. The grain adds a crisp, clean finish without imparting much flavor. It simultaneously lightens the body and increases the ABV.

*TRY: **ASAHI SUPER DRY, THE BRUERY TRADE WINDS TRIPEL***

BEST BEER PRACTICES

Do you know how to shop for beer? I don't mean grabbing a six-pack off the shelf and exchanging it for money—anyone with enough years behind them or, ahem, a plausible ID can do that—but earnestly shopping for the best, freshest beer available? Like knowing which stores stock the freshest cans, have the highest turnover of inventory, or get the rarest selection of bottles?

Consumers are often overwhelmed with choice when they walk down the beer aisle. We've all been there, staring at row after row of beer, wondering which IPA to choose of the dozen or so available, trying to guess and conjure flavors based on terse descriptions and flowery language. It can get downright tiresome.

To help you get the best beer available, here are suggestions on how and where to shop for beer, and which beers to buy where. Of course, this all depends on where you live and what you have access to, but let's assume you have a local supermarket, a bottle shop, a brewery, and access to the web.

FIVE TIPS FOR
EXPERT BEER SHOPPING

1. BUY THE FRESHEST BEER POSSIBLE.
Often that means choosing regional or local beers over imports or national brands, and favoring stores with high turnover to ones whose inventory doesn't move quickly.

2. NOTICE HOW THE BEER IS KEPT.
Most beer should be stored cool or cold, and all beer should be kept out of direct sunlight. If you see a store with bottles in direct sunlight, avoid shopping there.

3. SHOP AT DIFFERENT LOCATIONS FOR DIFFERENT BEERS.
Different outlets specialize in different styles and products, and nearly all retailers have their strengths and weaknesses. Use this variety to your advantage.

4. CHECK THE DATE CODE.
Know how to locate a beer's code, indicating when the beer was bottled. If you spot an expired or out-of-date beer on the shelf, don't shop there.

5. DON'T BE AFRAID TO ASK QUESTIONS.
Even if you shop for beer at a grocery store, chances are the person in charge of ordering that beer can answer your questions. At bottle shops or breweries the staff will be more than willing to geek out with you on hops or provide precise recommendations for bottles and styles.

WHERE TO SHOP

SUPERMARKETS

Large supermarkets are increasingly decent options for purchasing good beer. Most stock the big national and international brands, and move through inventory quickly. They also stock national and regional craft beer, and may even offer a selection from local breweries. Often, you can mix and match six packs of individual bottles or cans, a great option for testing new beers without committing to an entire six-pack or case.

WHAT TO BUY: MIXED SIX PACKS; NATIONAL AND REGIONAL CRAFT BEERS; MACROBREWS IN QUANTITY

A bottle store in Ghent, Belgium

BOTTLE SHOPS

Specialty beer shops typically have a wider, more diverse selection than supermarkets. They stock beer from small, esoteric breweries and are staffed by knowledgeable, passionate beer geeks. (Shop at one enough and you'll likely develop a rapport with the staff, which comes in handy for special releases and when you're seeking new recommendations.) Some even offer draft beer to go in glass jugs called growlers or large, single-use cans called Crowlers™—the beer is poured and sealed to order. A popular twist on this model is the bottle shop–cum–beer bar, which allows drinkers to knock back pints on premise and take beer to go.

WHAT TO BUY: ESOTERIC BOTTLES; SPECIAL RELEASES; GROWLERS AND CROWLERS™

BREWERIES

For the freshest beer, go straight to the source. Most breweries sell beer directly to imbibers, either in a tasting room or retail shop. And even if your local spot doesn't offer packaged, bottled, or canned beers, most will fill a growler for you to take home. A bonus? Since the intermediary is removed, you'll pay the lowest prices, while directly supporting a local business.

WHAT TO BUY: PINTS IN THE TASTING ROOM; RARE AND ONE-OFF RELEASES; GROWLERS AND CROWLERS™

ONLINE

The explosion of online beer sellers means many once hard-to-find bottles are just a click or two away. Of course, delivery depends on whether your municipality allows delivery of alcohol, but

BREW BY - 21/09
NUMBERS   NZ PALE   £16.50

MAD HATTER - TZATZIKI   £14
                 SOUR

Growlers in Bison Beer Crafthouse, Brighton, UK

for the most part, beer from far-flung locales is no longer necessarily difficult to acquire. Be sure to order from a reputable source, though—some online retailers stock old, stale beer that's spent far too much time collecting dust in the warehouse.

WHAT TO BUY: *BEER NOT DISTRIBUTED TO YOUR REGION; VINTAGE BEER; HARD-TO-FIND BOTTLES*

VINTAGE BEER

Although you should avoid expired or out-of-date beer for most styles, that isn't always the case. In fact, some beers improve with age. Age-able beers will keep for years, progressing and evolving right in the bottle.

DATE CODING

Most beer is tagged with a stamp indicating when it was packaged or when it is best consumed by. These are called date codes, and if you know how to spot and decode them, they can help you purchase the freshest beer possible.

Date codes vary wildly across breweries and locales, and deciphering them can be tricky. The most straightforward ones will clearly state the day, month, and year on which the beer was packaged. Others indicate a "Best By" date, which typically means 90 to 120 days after packaging. The worst examples use cryptic Julian calendar dates that indicate the numbered day of the year followed by the last digit in the year. For example, a beer packaged on February 1, 2017, would obtain the code "0327". Other codes are notched on the label, indicating with a tick mark or small groove the month and day on which the beer was packaged. Some beers have no date code at all.

SERVING TEMPERATURE

These are temperatures at which different types of beer should be poured. Inevitably, the liquid will warm in the glass as you sip, which is a good thing, because it encourages flavors to unfurl and evolve.

55°F : IMPERIAL PORTER AND STOUT BARLEYWINE BELGIAN QUAD

45°F: SAISON AND FARMHOUSE PORTER AND STOUT IPA

40°F : PILSNER AND LIGHT LAGER PALE ALE KÖLSCH

BUILDING YOUR OWN BEER CELLAR

Now that you know how to shop for the best beer available, it's time to think about how to keep it. For beer intended to be consumed fresh, nothing's better than a standard 40°F refrigerator. Kept in such conditions and consumed within a few weeks or up to a month, the beer should taste vibrant and bright. But for beer you plan to age, you'll want a dark, cool environment that fosters flavor development and evolution.

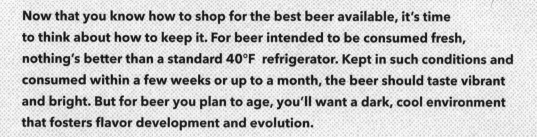

WHY AGE BEER?

Aging encourages beer's inherent flavors to expand and evolve right inside the bottle, resulting in a transformed, multilayered, and (hopefully!) delicious brew. Part of the fun of collecting beer is tasting it during an arch of evolution. There's no better way to do that than with a home cellar.

BUILDING YOUR INVENTORY

What are the best beers to stock in your cellar? In general, if it's dark and boozy, you can age it. Think barleywines, Russian imperial stouts, and Trappist quads. Sour ales with funky bacteria—Belgian lambics, for example—age remarkably well, too, as do many saisons and farmhouse ales inoculated with Brettanomyces. In fact, nearly all sours are good candidates for aging because the yeast will continue to develop and alter the beer's flavors while the bottle is being stored.

This may sound ridiculously obvious, but avoid aging beers that are best consumed fresh—that means light, delicate ones like pilsners and fresh IPAs. Their ephemeral aromas and flavors dissipate within weeks and are all but obliterated after months. That's not to say they won't taste good after a prolonged sojourn in the cellar; they just won't be at their prime.

CONSTRUCTING YOUR CELLARING SPACE

An ideal aging environment is a cool, dark spot with a constant temperature of around 55°F. If you're fortunate enough to have a natural space like this at your disposal—say, an actual real-life below ground cellar—by all means, use it to age beer. But if, like me, you live in a minuscule apartment with nary a shelf to spare, you'll need to be more imaginative.

A decent cellaring space can be as simple as a box in the back of a closet. Or it can be a high-tech climate-controlled room. You're likely to settle for something in between, but regardless of scale and scope, a handful of factors are common to creating a friendly beer-aging situation.

First, the space should be dark. Direct sunlight initiates a chemical reaction in beer that causes it to "skunk." Second, it should be in the Goldilocks zone of temperatures: neither too cold nor too hot. Fridge-like conditions inhibit beer's ability to evolve over time, while high temperatures and wild fluctuations can lead to off flavors.

The position in which your bottles are stored is another consideration. Some breweries age their beers horizontally, but for home collectors, storing your bottles upright is the best practice. (This minimizes the surface area of beer exposed to oxygen that may be in the bottle.)

HOW TO GET STARTED

Set a budget for both beer and equipment. If you can afford a wine fridge, buy one. If not, find a space in your home that's dark and cool where the beer can be kept pretty much undisturbed for months or even years.

SCRATCH AND SNIFF! Beer can be stored in barrels that once held whiskey

Then buy as many different bottles as you can. Stock up on multiples of a single beer—part of the fun of cellaring is tasting and tracking a beer as it ages over time. I recommend buying three bottles of any beer you intend to cellar. Open one bottle immediately and make notes on how it tastes. In six months, open another bottle and describe how it's changed. This should give you a good perspective on how the beer might evolve going forward. The third you can keep for as long as you like, up to several years.

Remember: longer is not necessarily better. Two to four years is usually the maximum for storing most beers, though some are excellent at five and even ten years of age. As soon as you think the beer is not as good as the last time you drank it, it's probably not going to rebound. At that point it's time to sup up and drink the rest of those beers.

FIVE BEERS TO GET YOU STARTED

STONE ENJOY AFTER–BRETT IPA

IPAs conditioned with Brettanomyces are suitable for aging. Developed as an antidote to the brewery's ultra-fresh Enjoy By series, this is primed with Brettanomyces and intended for aging for many months past the Enjoy After date.

SIERRA NEVADA BIGFOOT–AMERICAN BARLEYWINE

Bigfoot is the everyman of aged beer—inexpensive, available at many supermarkets, and fortified with huge quantities of malt and hops whose flavors become robust and sherry-like over time.

RODENBACH GRAND CRU–FLANDERS RED ALE

This Belgian Flanders red is a blend of young and aged beer. Its flavors are tart, fruity, and complex with a smooth finish that only gets softer and richer with age.

BOON OUDE GEUZE MARIAGE PARFAIT–GEUZE

This supremely tart 100 percent spontaneous ale blends young and old lambic. It's zesty with flavors of green apple, lemon, and hay. Brewed with aged hops, it will mature and evolve beautifully for many years.

FIRESTONE WALKER PARABOLA–RUSSIAN IMPERIAL STOUT

Nearly all imperial stouts are suitable for aging, but this one is a favorite. The beer is aged for a year in bourbon barrels before bottling. With age, the alcohol mellows and the beer becomes velvety and chocolaty, with notes of vanilla and charred oak.

BEER

GLASSWARE

Order a draft beer at nearly any bar or restaurant and chances are it will be delivered in a 16- or 20-oz, thick-walled, slightly downward-tapering shaker glass. It's the world's most ubiquitous beer glass because it's easy to stack and difficult to break, making it a favorite for bartenders and bar owners alike.

Unfortunately, it also happens to be one of the worst vessels for tasting beer. First, the wide mouth dissipates rather than concentrates the beer's aromas, making the beer smell flat and insipid. Second, its thick walls deliver the liquid to all the wrong areas rather than guiding it to the sweet center of your palate. This is okay for some beers, but the one-size-fits-all pint just won't cut it.

So, what are the best glasses to use? It depends on the beer. Lighter ones like pilsners, wheat ales, and most IPAs are best dispensed into a tall glass with a slight taper at the brim. Rich, intensely flavored beers like barrel-aged stouts and barleywines are partial to squat, bulbous snifters—the kind your grandfather might have sipped Scotch from.

The market is flooded with options, so here are a few general guidelines to keep in mind when buying glasses for your home:

CHOOSE VERSATILITY OVER SPECIFICITY

Some companies market glasses for each style like IPAs, stouts, wheat beers, and pilsners. While most of these are well crafted and elegant, they simply aren't necessary and will inevitably crowd your cupboards. Choose two or three versatile glasses you can use across a range of styles and flavors.

THINK SLEEK AND CLASSIC, NOT CLUMSY AND TRENDY

A classic thin-lipped wineglass will get way more beer mileage in my house than a dimpled mug or shaker pint. And unless you're throwing a rowdy Oktoberfest rager, don't even think about dusting off the beer boot!

These tulip-shaped beer glasses are ready and waiting

THREE GLASSES TO OWN

WILLI BECHER GLASS The Willi Becher glass is a German design most commonly used for pilsners and other light, sessionable beers. It comes in a variety of sizes, but the 500 ml (16 oz) is best for most lagers, IPAs, and everyday porters and stouts. The slight conical taper at the top concentrates flavors and projects bright, fresh aromas from the light surface directly to your olfactory zones.

- -

CLASSIC WINEGLASS No, it isn't pretentious to put beer in a wineglass! Especially if you're drinking a fruity, effervescent saison from Belgium or a light-bodied simple sour from Germany or the US. Not only is it the perfect size for beer (comfortably holding around 8 to 10 oz of liquid), the stem prevents your hand from warming the beer as you hold it. Need more proof? Basic wineglasses are increasingly the go-to stemware at serious beer bars throughout the world.

- -

SNIFTER GLASS For big beers like imperial stouts, barleywines, and Belgian quads, choose a snifter glass. Strong, aggressive flavors require small pours at relatively warm temperatures (around 55°F). This makes them perfectly suited for a round, short-stemmed snifter like the kind used for bourbon, brandy, or cognac. The balloon shape focuses volatile aromas that would otherwise dissipate in an open-topped glass, while allowing the beer to unfurl and develop as it warms in the glass.

AND ONE GLASS THAT CAN DO EVERYTHING...

If you had to choose one glass that works for every beer style imaginable, from the lightest lagers to the burliest barleywines, it would be the Spiegelau Beer Tulip. It's the most versatile glassware in the world, with a thin rim and a generous but tapered shape that makes practically any beer you pour into it seem like a revelation. It combines the best traits of the three glasses into a single vessel.

A BEER-TASTING PRIMER

Now that you know how to shop for, store, and serve beer, it's finally time to taste it! Hurrah! Here, we break beer tasting down into five primary components for consideration when evaluating beer.

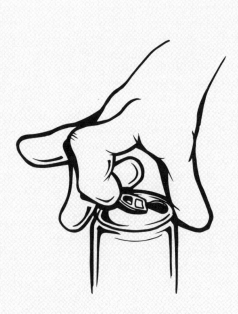

First, though, you've got to get it into the glass. The best way to pour beer is to tilt your glass at a 45° angle and pour slowly against the glass's wall. As you pour, gradually bring the vessel upright and finish with a parting shot directly in the center of the liquid. Be sure to leave some room in your glass for sniffing—don't fill it all the way up!

Note: Most beer is gassed to a normal Budweiser-level carbonation, but some—especially saisons, farmhouse ales, and mixed-culture beers—can have very high levels of carbon dioxide. Sometimes they even gush out of the bottle when the cap or cork is pulled! (These are called gushers.) Open these styles over or near a sink in case of eruption. Such beer may also contain yeast sediment at the bottom or along the length of the bottle, depending on how it's been stored. Don't drink the sediment if you don't want to, but know that's it's full of good-for-you nutrients and Vitamins B1, B2, and B12.

NOW IT'S TIME TO TASTE.

Evaluate the clarity of the beer by holding it up to the light

1. LOOK AT THE BEER. Hold it up to a light. Notice its color and clarity. Is it hazy and cloudy or bright and clear? Does it have a fluffy, cloud-like head or a thin, soapy film? Does the liquid itself look clean? Is there anything particularly unusual about its appearance? (Is it hot pink or magenta, for instance? If so, it probably contains fruits or flowers.) Make notes or describe it to a friend.

2. SMELL IT. Get your nose in there, breathe deeply and inhale with your lips shut. Swirl it around the glass a little so that more aromas are released. Then sniff it again. Keep doing this until you're ready to taste it. Think about what you're smelling and describe it to a friend.

3. TASTE IT. Sip the beer and hold it in your mouth. Don't swish it around the way you would wine or mouthwash, but think about it and consider what flavors you're tasting. Breathe through your nose and notice how the beer is changing. "Chew" on it some more and then swallow. What's the finish like? Does it taste the same or remarkably different from the first sip? Note what flavors you've experienced and how the taste changes over time.

4. FEEL IT. Did the beer seem viscous and sticky on your palate or was it thin and watery? Maybe somewhere in between? Was it spicy and prickly at all, or creamy and smooth? Maybe there was little or no carbonation. All these factors can indicate what base grains were used, how boozy the beer is, and how it was fermented.

5. OVERALL IMPRESSIONS ARE IMPORTANT. Do you like it? If so, can you describe why? Or did it literally leave a bad taste in your mouth? Did all the components sing together in harmony or did one or two stick out like a squeaky wheel?

GRAINS OF TRUTH

Have *you* properly soaked up this chapter's pearls of wisdom on how best to store beer and savor its flavor? To find out what you've learned—and how well you've learned it—pick out which of the following statements are *true or false* . . .

1. NO BEER EVER IMPROVES WITH AGE.

2. IF YOUR STORE OR CELLAR IS REGULARLY EXPOSED TO DIRECT SUNLIGHT, THAT'S ABSOLUTELY FINE.

3. IT'S BEST TO STORE BOTTLES UPRIGHT RATHER THAN HORIZONTALLY.

4. THICK-WALLED, TAPERING SHAKER GLASSES ARE SOME OF THE BEST FOR HELPING YOU PICK UP BEER FLAVORS.

5. YOU ONLY REALLY NEED THREE VERSATILE TYPES OF BEER GLASS IN YOUR KITCHEN TO COVER THE FLAVOR SPECTRUM.

6. IT'S A VERY BAD IDEA—NOT TO MENTION PRETENTIOUS—TO DRINK BEER FROM A WINE GLASS.

7. THE SPIEGELAU BEER TULIP IS THE MOST VERSATILE GLASS IN THE WORLD.

8. SAISONS, FARMHOUSE ALES, AND MIXED-CULTURE BEERS TEND TO HAVE LOW LEVELS OF CARBON DIOXIDE, SO THEY'RE QUITE UNLIKELY TO GUSH ON YOU.

9. AVOID DRINKING SEDIMENT AT ALL COSTS. I MEAN, BLEURGH—THERE'S NO NUTRITIONAL OR FLAVOR VALUE IN IT WHATSOEVER.

10. A HOT PINK OR MAGENTA TONE THROUGHOUT A BEER USUALLY SIGNALS FRUIT OR FLOWER CONTENT.

11. THE STRONG, AGGRESSIVE FLAVORS OF IMPERIAL STOUTS AND BARLEYWINES ARE BEST ENJOYED FROM SMALLER POURS.

12. OPEN-TOPPED GLASSES HELP YOU GET THE MOST OUT OF VOLATILE AROMAS BY SETTING THEM FREE.

13. PALE ALE SHOULD IDEALLY BE SERVED AT AROUND 55°F.

14. IPAS ARE BEST SERVED AT AROUND 45°F.

15. BOTTLED BEERS ARE THE BEST ONES TO DRINK IN A NICE, HOT SHOWER.

Solution on page 159

SHOWER BEERS

One of the simplest pleasurable acts in the world is enjoying an ice-cold beer while taking a steaming hot shower. Indulgent? Yes. Gratifying? Absolutely. Uncouth? Definitely. But you're an adult, and you make your own decisions.

Whether it's to unwind after a hard day's work or to pregame for a big night out, the unadulterated delight in this basic but satisfying act is simply unparalleled. Here are some guidelines for optimizing your shower sipper.

1. CAN IT. Showers are slippery, slick places full of liquids, lotions, soaps, and suds. So grab a canned beer instead of a bottle. Cans are easier to grip anyway, and if you happen to drop your beer—a severe enough tragedy in and of itself—at least you won't wind up with a bathtub full of shattered glass.

2. CHOOSE LIGHT. Unless you're really trying to pregame hard, stick with a beer below 5 percent ABV and you're much less likely to stumble out of the shower.

3. MAKE IT A TREAT. Shower beers should be an occasional treat, not part of your daily grooming routine. Although it may be tempting to indulge on a regular basis, the novelty will quickly wear off if you make it a regular occurrence.

4. TAKE YOUR TIME. That said, when you do indulge, take your time! After all, this is supposed to be a pleasurable, satisfying act. Your olfactory senses will already be heightened from the steam and multifarious shower smells, so it's a great opportunity to meditate on your beer's qualities.

SO GO AHEAD–TREAT YOURSELF– AND GRAB A SHOWER BEER NEXT TIME YOU'RE ABOUT TO SLIP BEHIND THE CURTAIN.

DOWN THE GULLET

The beer question I get asked second most often—behind "What's your favorite beer?"—is, "How do you match beer with food?" It's a loaded one that unfortunately doesn't have a simple answer.

Some of it boils down to personal preference, but there are a few widely accepted tenets for making a harmonious marriage between good food and good beer.

If you're familiar with pairing wine with food, you'll already know the two overarching flavor theories of contrasting and complementary. Complementary means pairing drink and food in such a way that similar flavors highlight and enhance one another—

pairing like with like. Contrasting flavors, on the other hand, work because they are dissimilar, standing in direct contrast to one another—salty and sweet, for instance, or fatty and acidic. Think salted caramels or Carolina-style pork barbecue with a vinegary sauce. With beer, this could mean pairing briny oysters on the half shell with robust dark Irish stout. Or a fatty sausage with a tart Berliner weisse.

Of course, there are overlaps with complementary and contrasting flavors—they're rarely mutually exclusive. In fact, contrasting flavors and textures complement one another because they highlight and temper their disparate characteristics. It can be confusing. And believe me, nearly everyone struggles with it. But stick with a few general guidelines, and you'll soon be enjoying your favorite brew alongside the perfect culinary partner.

TIPS ON BEER AND FOOD PAIRING

PAIR LIGHT WITH LIGHT. Light-colored beers like witbier, hefeweizen, and cream ale pair well with light-colored foods—ricotta toast with honey, raw and gently cooked seafood, weisswurst, and light pasta dishes.

SAISONS ARE GOOD ALL-ROUND BEERS. Saisons and farmhouse ales are the versatile workhorses of beer and food pairings. They often have a dry finish that's refreshing and palate cleansing with each sip, and their earthy flavors pair well with a wide range of dishes from light salads and crudités to roasted chicken and grilled pork tenderloin.

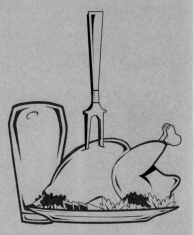

DRINK PILSNERS AND PALE LAGERS WITH SPICY FOOD. My go-to for spicy dishes and other aggressive flavors is always a pilsner or light, international lager. They are practically the only beers consumed in countries with high-heat index cooking because they are thirst-quenching and refreshing. Most of all, they don't compete with the flavor, heat, and spice—they play a supporting role.

FINISH STRONG. Like sherry and port, strong beers are best reserved for the end of a meal when the night is winding down and your stomach needs settling. They pair well with sweet foods and help with digestion.

BEER & FOOD PAIRING

Food pairing isn't just for wine enthusiasts—it's also an essential skill for any beer expert. Follow the lines to discover which brew will perfectly enhance your favorite dish.

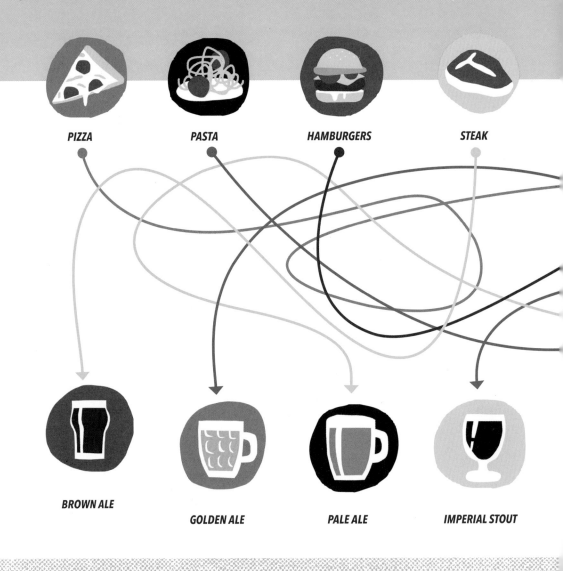

PIZZA   PASTA   HAMBURGERS   STEAK

BROWN ALE   GOLDEN ALE   PALE ALE   IMPERIAL STOUT

Beer and a burger? Yes please! But which beer? Almost any beer and food pairing should work well. But some beers can be paired with food to get a particularly delicious result. Light and fruity wheat beers provide an incredible sweet pairing to play off against salty food. Pilsners and lagers provide a refreshing companion to greasy food like pizza; heavier ales, rich in malt, go well with steaks. The possibilities are endless and it is all about experimenting. Follow the mazes below to discover some excellent combinations to start your food pairing journey.

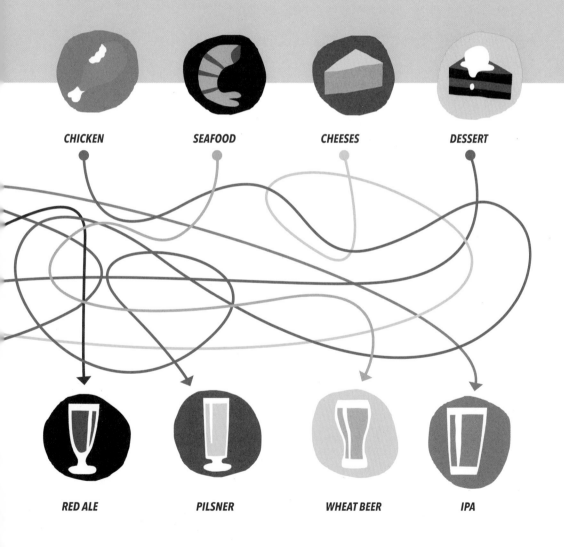

CHICKEN   SEAFOOD   CHEESES   DESSERT

RED ALE   PILSNER   WHEAT BEER   IPA

HEAR YE, HEAR YE!
IPAS DO NOT BELONG AT THE DINNER TABLE

There's an old bit of food and beer pairing wisdom that posits spicy dishes love hoppy beers. The truth, it turns out, is that hops accentuate spiciness, meaning IPAs and other hoppy beers are actually the worst ones for spicy dishes. When paired with spicy food they are not refreshing, they are not thirst-quenching, they are not palate-cleansing—they simply do not belong anywhere near spicy foods.

In fact, modern IPAs rarely pair well with any food. Their citrusy, piney, floral flavors are simply too aggressive, too palate coating, and too manifold to work with most food. IPAs entirely miss the mark of pairing beer and food—they don't make food taste better and the food doesn't make them taste better. That's why I say forget IPAs when it comes to food.

That said, I'll concede a couple of food scenarios where IPAs and other hoppy beers are not horrible matches with food. My favorite is grilled hot dogs. Because hot dogs are a singular, robust flavor, they present a rare chance for IPAs to shine in a setting where they don't interfere or strike discord with complex tastes and aromas. Another good pairing is IPAs and salty potato chips.

Pair IPAs with grilled hot dogs

You might notice a correlation here—IPAs tend to pair well with junk foods you would more likely encounter on the couch, at a bar, or at a cookout than in the dining room or at a restaurant table.

BEER RECIPES

Cooking with beer should be a fun experience, but it should also be a deliberate act—dumping a bottle of light lager into a big vat of dark-red chile hardly qualifies! Think about what you want to get out of the beer before adding it to a dish. Do you want to impart the beer's flavor to the overall taste? Do you want to add steam and moisture? How's color going to influence the finished product? These are considerations to weigh up before you get started.

Beer can be used in any number of dishes, sometimes as a substitute for wine, but more often as a flavor component itself. Here are some tips:

1. BEER IS A FLAVOR COMPONENT, not just a liquid. This might seem painfully obvious, but when a recipe calls for "beer," you'll need to consider what other flavors are going on in there and how the beer you choose will interact with everything else.

2. BEER IS INHERENTLY BITTER and becomes ever more so when it reduces. So be sure to add some sweet element—sugar, honey, carrots—when braising with it. And stay away from super-bitter styles like American IPAs.

3. TASTE A HANDFUL OF BEERS to understand the character and flavors the beer will impart to your dish. Be critical—if you don't like the beer, chances are you won't like what it does to your food.

A yeast bread works well flavored with beer

BEER CAN CHICKEN

Beer Can Chicken is a staple of summertime barbecues and cookouts throughout the US, particularly in the South. The idea is simple—grill-roast a whole, dry-rubbed bird set vertically atop a beer can until the meat is moist and tender. The beer supposedly evaporates keeping the chicken moist while it cooks.

SINCE THE BEER DOESN'T IMPART MUCH FLAVOR TO THE CHICKEN, USE ANY BEER YOU'D LIKE. IF YOU'RE WORRIED ABOUT THE BISPHENOL A LINING IN BEER CANS, USE A VERTICAL ROASTING STAND INSTEAD—THEY CAN BE PURCHASED AT MANY HARDWARE AND KITCHEN SUPPLY STORES. ALSO, FEEL FREE TO ADJUST THE DRY-RUB FORMULA AS YOU LIKE. THIS ONE IS TRADITIONAL, BUT PRACTICALLY ANY KIND OF MEAT SEASONING WOULD BE TASTY.

- -

INGREDIENTS

FOR THE DRY RUB
1 tbsp salt
1 tbsp pepper
1 tbsp granulated white sugar
1 tbsp light-brown sugar
1 tbsp coriander
2 tbsp cumin
2 tbsp chile powder
3 tbsp smoked paprika

FOR THE CHICKEN
1 whole chicken, neck and giblets removed, about 4 to 5 lbs total
1 beer can
Barbecue sauce or other basting liquid (optional)

METHOD

1. Mix all ingredients for the dry-rub in a bowl. Pat the chicken dry with paper towels and coat it inside and out with the dry-rub. Let it rest until your grill is ready.

2. Heat a grill so that half the grilling area is hot and the other is merely warm. (If using a charcoal grill, push all the coals on one side; if using gas, turn one side to high and leave the other side turned off.)

3. Drink or pour half the beer from the can so that it's half full. On a level surface, slide the bird over the beer can so that its inner thighs straddle the can and its cavity is stuffed. Balance the can-stuffed bird on the cool side of the grates and cover the grill.

4. Cook until the breast meat registers 165°F, about an hour to an hour and a half. Baste with barbecue sauce or other basting liquid throughout the cooking process, especially toward the end of cooking.

5. Rest the bird at least fifteen minutes before removing the beer can (caution: it may be hot!) and carving.

BEER CHEESE

Beer Cheese is readily available at most supermarkets, but try
making your own with leftover scraps from last night's cheese plate.
You can use pretty much any fresh or soft cheese, as long as it's not a hard or
aged one. You'll need about 12 oz total, softened to room temperature, to
which you'll add a little garlic, salt, paprika, and—of course—a splash of beer.
Served with some toasted bread, a handful of crackers, and a few pickled
veggies on the side, it's one of the best beer snacks there ever was.

*NOTE: USE ANY LIGHT-COLORED BEER YOU LIKE, BUT A CZECH-STYLE PILSNER LIKE
PILSNER URQUELL IS OUR FAVORITE. IT'S AROMATIC, FLORAL, AND SPRIGHTLY ENOUGH
TO CUT THROUGH THE RICHNESS OF THE DAIRY.*

- -

INGREDIENTS

¾ bottle/can of beer, such as Czech pilsner,
Kölsch, or a light, not-too-hoppy pale ale

12 oz mixed soft cheese at room temperature—
a blend of blue cheese, quark, farmer's cheese,
and/or Neufchâtel works perfectly

Generous pinch of paprika

Small clove of garlic, grated or minced

Generous pinch of salt

METHOD

1. Whisk the beer in a bowl until most of the carbonation is lost and the beer is flat. Alternatively, heat it in a pot on the stove for the same effect. Combine the flat beer with all remaining ingredients in a food processor and process until smooth and creamy.

2. Line a mesh kitchen strainer with a dampened cheesecloth. Place the beer cheese mixture in the lined strainer and cover the top with plastic wrap. Set over a shallow bowl and let strain overnight in the fridge.

3. Uncover, remove the cheese from the strainer, and set on a plate or in a bowl. Sprinkle with paprika, garlic, and a pinch of fancy, flaky salt like Maldon. Serve alongside toasted baguette slices, crackers, pickled veggies, and crudités.

Stainless-steel beer kegs at the Great American Beer Festival. Each year, GABF represents the largest collection of US beer ever served, in a public tasting event plus a private competition. Founded in 1982, GABF has been growing along with the American craft brewing industry ever since.

BEER-CANDIED
BACON

Candied bacon is a super-simple snack that comes together with just four ingredients—bacon, brown sugar, cayenne pepper, and beer. You toss it in the oven, brush it with a little beer-sugar-cayenne mixture, *et voila*: one of the easiest, most delicious and crowd-pleasing snacks you can make.

FOR EXTRA-SMOKY FLAVOR TO MATCH THE INTENSITY OF THE BACON,
TRY A RAUCHBIER FOR THE GLAZE.

- -

INGREDIENTS

1 lb thick-sliced bacon
⅓ cup light-brown sugar
¼ tsp cayenne pepper
½ bottle robust dark ale like a brown ale,
porter, or stout

METHOD

1. Preheat oven to 400°F. Whisk the sugar, cayenne, and beer in a small saucepan over medium heat. Cook for five or six minutes to form a thin glaze. (The beer will foam, but will naturally settle after a few minutes.) Allow to cool slightly.

2. Place a wire rack over a rimmed baking sheet. Dip the bacon slices in the glaze and place on top of the rack in a single layer (work in batches if you need to).

3. Cook for fifteen minutes, then flip and brush the bacon with more glaze. Repeat two to three more times until the bacon is crisp, sticky, and brown.

4. Cool on the wire rack for at least thirty minutes before serving.

BLACK
VELVET

This classic mixed cocktail merges champagne with dark stout beer, two flavors that complement each other. It was first created in 1831 by Brook's gentlemen's club in London to symbolize mourning, following the death of Prince Albert.

A DARK STOUT LIKE GUINNESS EXTRA STOUT IS THE BEST TYPE OF BEER TO USE IN THIS COCKTAIL.

INGREDIENTS

½ glass chilled champagne or prosecco
¼ glass dark stout beer

METHOD

Half fill champagne flutes with dark stout beer, then slowly top them up with chilled champagne or prosecco. Achieve layering by pouring each over the back of a spoon down the sides of the glass.

FLAMING
DR. PEPPER

This drink is a shooter—one to drink down in one gulp—and it tastes just like Dr. Pepper. This is quite a strong drink, so you'll want to limit yourself to one (or maybe two) a night.

USE A WHEAT ALE LIKE A BELGIAN WITBIER FOR THIS ONE—THERE'S SOMETHING ABOUT THE BANANA AND CLOVE NOTES IN WITBIER THAT REALLY WORKS WITH AND ECHOES THE ROBUST SPICY FLAVORS OF THE RUM AND AMARETTO.

INGREDIENTS

½ glass beer
¾ shot amaretto liqueur
¼ shot rum

METHOD

1. Half fill a pint glass with beer.
2. Pour the amaretto into a standard shot glass. Slowly pour the rum on top of the amaretto, so that it floats.
3. Carefully set the shot on fire, by touching it with an open flame.
4. Drop the lit shot into the half-full glass of beer and slam it down on the table.

CAUTION: ALWAYS TAKE GREAT CARE WHEN DEALING WITH AN OPEN FLAME!

MILK STOUT
ICE CREAM

Stouts are an easy decision when it comes to dessert, as they contain all the flavors of dessert right in the glass—chocolate, coffee, and lactose sugar—making them perfect ingredients for baking. They work seamlessly in myriad dessert recipes like flourless chocolate cakes, stout brownies, and even Guinness floats.

THIS MILK STOUT ICE CREAM IS A SIMPLE PREPARATION PROVIDED YOU HAVE THE RIGHT TOOLS. INVEST IN AN ICE-CREAM MACHINE IF YOU CAN AFFORD ONE—IT WILL SAVE YOU MONEY OVERALL, ESPECIALLY IF YOU'RE A WEEKLY ICE-CREAM EATER.

- -

INGREDIENTS

7 oz semi-sweet or milk chocolate
1 cup whole milk
½ cup sugar
Pinch of salt
4 egg yolks
1 cup heavy cream
¾ cup milk stout (like Stone Xocoveza)
1 tsp vanilla extract

Go crazy with whatever stout you'd like here. We like Stone's Xocoveza, which is a winter seasonal mocha stout with lactose, coffee, spices, and chile peppers that adds a beguiling twist to the ice cream. Imperial stouts could work here, too, though you may need to add an ounce or two more to make up for its thick, viscous consistency. Serve plain, with your favorite toppings, or as a beer float. Alternatively, top a scoop with a shot of espresso for a fun take on an *affogato*.

METHOD

1. Finely chop the chocolate and put in a bowl.

2. Gently warm the milk, sugar, and salt in a saucepan. Whisk the egg yolks in a separate bowl and slowly pour in the warm milk mixture. Return it all to the saucepan and heat until thickened.

3. Pour the hot milk and egg mixture over the chocolate and whisk until the chocolate is completely incorporated and melted. Stir in the cream, stout, and vanilla.

4. Chill in the refrigerator overnight. Follow the manufacturer's instructions for freezing the mixture in an ice-cream maker. Serve with a tall glass of the same stout, or make a stout float with beer and ice cream.

WHICH BEER AM I?

We asked nine beer types to tell you a few things about themselves, without completely revealing who they are. Can you guess which variety each brew is? Oh, and by the way, the answers aren't just within this chapter!

1. "I'M A STRONG, SWEET, AND SLIGHTLY SYRUPY SIDEKICK TO A DESSERT–OR JUST A WINNING WAY TO CAP OFF A FILLING MEAL, IF YOUR STOMACH NEEDS SETTLING."

2. "I AM YOUR FIRE EXTINGUISHER IN THE FACE OF FLAMING FLAVORS. NEED AN ALLY TO DOUSE DOWN SOME SPICES AND PUT AGGRESSIVE TASTES IN THEIR PLACE? WELL, I'M YOUR BEER."

3. "I'M THE PALATE CLEANSER. I HAVE A REFRESHING, DRY TANG THAT'S SURE TO KEEP YOU ALERT WHEN YOU CHOW DOWN, AND IF YOU HAVE SOME GRILLED CHICKEN OR PORK TENDERLOIN AROUND, I'LL HIT IT OFF WITH THEM JUST FINE."

4. "TO BE SURE, I CAN THINK OF NOTHING BETTER THAN WRAPPING MY DARK, ROBUST FLAVOR SPECTRUM AROUND A BRINY OYSTER OR TWO!"

5. "IT'S NOT THAT I'M SLUMMING IT OR ANYTHING–IT'S JUST THAT I CAN ONLY SEEM TO MAKE FRIENDS WITH STUFF LIKE HOT DOGS OR POTATO CHIPS. AH WELL, SOMEONE HAS TO BE JUNK FOOD'S BEST PAL–MIGHT AS WELL BE ME."

6. "IF YOU'RE WHIPPING UP A FLEMISH BEEF STEW AND WANT A LITTLE SWEET-AND-SOUR TOUCH, YOU COULD DO A LOT WORSE THAN POUR ME IN THE MIX–ALTHOUGH MAYBE I SHOULDN'T BE TALKING TO YOU, BECAUSE OF MY VOWS AND STUFF."

7. "MY ARISTOCRATIC REPUTATION IS ONE OF A HARDY VOYAGER WHO WAS BREWED IN LONDON, THEN SHIPPED OUT TO RUSSIA'S MONARCHY AND THE BALTIC STATES–BUT SOMEONE MAY HAVE MADE ALL THAT UP. ONE THING'S FOR SURE, MY FLAVOR'S SO FOCUSED, IT'S DOUBLE-CONCENTRATED."

8. "IF YOU'RE LOOKING FOR THE PERFECT TOAST FOR A PERFECT ROAST, I'M THE ONLY GAME IN TOWN. THE FLAVORS OF CARAMELIZED ONIONS, OVEN-SOFTENED VEGETABLES, AND SUCCULENT CHICKEN GET A REAL LIFT WHENEVER I'M AROUND."

9. "I AM A FLAVOR CHAMELEON, ELUSIVE AND UNUSUAL–AND YET RIGHT FROM THE HEART OF EUROPE. BOASTING AROMATIC TOUCHES OF CLOVE, BANANA, CORIANDER, AND ORANGE PEEL, I BRING A NOTE OF UNDERSTATED FLAMBOYANCE TO THE TABLE."

Solution on page 159

BEER COOKOUT
WHAT TO PAIR WITH YOUR BACKYARD GRILL

RAVE!

Besides IPA, what other beers should you serve with grilled foods? Pilsners are never a bad option in summertime. But for a more exciting, exacting pairing, try some of these!

GRILLED CHICKEN Brown ales and other beers with malt-forward flavors pair well with grilled chicken. The meat is essentially a blank canvas, so the dominant flavor is smoke, marinade, and char. Go with a fruity, yeast-driven beer like a Belgian dubbel.

GRILLED FISH Fish is a broad category, so go with a beer that is equally versatile and multifaceted. Saisons are a good option because they're bubbly, effervescent, and dry—they also pair well with shellfish and oysters.

SCRATCH AND
SNIFF!

Smoky, peaty ales pair well with meat

Backyard-grilled fish

CHARRED BURGERS Charred red meat needs some texture, so find a beer that will stand up to the meat. That doesn't necessarily mean high-alcohol or strong beers—try to find a beer with some chewiness and structure. Coffee stouts and robust porters are at the top of my list.

SMOKED BARBECUE Smoked meats need an equally robust beer to stand up to their heady flavors. I like malty, strong dark beers like Scotch ales with a barbecue. Many are slightly smoky and peaty, which matches perfectly with perfumed, fatty meat.

GRILLED SAUSAGES For light sausages, go with weissbier and pilsner. For meatier, porkier sausages, choose something heftier like a doppelbock.

ALTERNATE HOT DOG PAIRING Other than IPA, pair hot dogs with tart American-style goses. As these are light and refreshing, they pair well with fatty hot dogs.

STATE OF THE ARTS

Beer labels are the faces of packaged beer—they are our first impressions before trying a new brew, and the visual representations of beers we already know and love. But the idea of putting a paper label on a bottle of beer is a relatively new phenomenon, one that became popular over just the past hundred years or so.

Before paper labels became de rigueur, bottles were manufactured to include the brewery name, beer brand, and sometimes even artwork embossed on the bottle itself. Today, most beers contain paper labels, while some have artwork screen-printed or film-wrapped directly on the bottle. Many bottles contain more than one label. There's almost always one on the front with colorful art and design, but sometimes a back label or a neck label will be attached as well to give the bulk of the regulatory minutiae like the address of the brewery or bottler, government warnings, and even tasting notes and suggested food pairings.

Bottles align to reveal the Strutter rooster

Contemporary branding for LIC Beer Project, Queens, NY

Labels have come a long way over the years—they have become reflections of a company's ethos, philosophy, and personality. And they are serious business for the many graphic designers, artists, and illustrators who have made numerous beers look like outright works of art. Collecting beer labels is even a hobby to some beer drinkers, who enthusiastically collect vintage and rare cans, bottles, and labels.

Unfortunately, for every smartly designed, tasteful label, there seem to be an equal number of poorly drawn—or even vulgar—ones adorned with thinly veiled sexist or racist imagery and names ("Panty Dropper," "Once You Go Black," etc.). Of course, this type of mindless marketing and tacky art is nothing new for beer. Big companies like Budweiser and MillerCoors have long featured bikini-clad women as part of their advertising campaigns. Thankfully, today, most small, independent breweries are becoming more attuned with the ethos of their customer base and are placing an increasingly greater importance on stylish, attractive label artwork.

OMNIPOLLO BEER AND ART COLLECTIVE

Omnipollo is a Swedish beer and art collective founded in 2011 by brewer Henok Fentie and artist/designer Karl Grandin.

The mobile "brewery" follows the contract brewing or so-called gypsy model, utilizing existing breweries across the world to make their beer rather than maintaining their own facility. From the start, Omnipollo has placed a huge emphasis on art and design to go along with its awesome American-influenced craft beers—think bold, hoppy IPAs and strong imperial stouts.

The bottles themselves are works of art, adorned with all kinds of esoteric and colorful symbols often printed right onto the glass. Some of the most striking are Fatamorgana, an imperial wheat IPA; Agamemnon, an imperial stout; and Yellow Belly, a beer wrapped in white paper that evokes the image of a hooded Klansman. This label reads: "Yellow Belly—a person who is without courage, fortitude, or nerve; a coward."

THE CAN REVOLUTION

One of the biggest recent revolutions in beer artwork is a renewed interest in cans. What was once unhip and stodgy—a holdover from a bygone era of cheap, flavorless, mass-produced lagers—is now all the rage. Cans are outselling bottles, while providing a platform for expanded artwork and creativity.

As the saying goes, everything old is new again. Many of our dads collected beer cans. In college, we drank cheap swill from cans before tossing the crumpled aluminum into a recycling bin. But at some point, cans fell out of favor and bottles became the sophisticated beer vessels of choice.

Now the pendulum has swung back. While bottles are still most popular among independent and craft brewers, shelf space is increasingly being turned over to cans. Not only are cans better than bottles for keeping beer fresh, they also provide the perfect format for colorful, brash artwork. Many cans are printed full bleed, meaning the entire can is printed with a colorful image or

scene. Some cans are cartoonish and funny, while others are beautiful and striking with clever designs that just feel right in your hand. Beer cans have made a comeback in a very big way.

Don't hide your face when sipping from a can!

NO FAUX PAS: DRINK FROM THE CAN!

To drink or not to drink from the can—that is the question. Unless you're conducting a serious tasting or want to note the visual attributes of a beer like color and clarity, I say there's absolutely nothing wrong with sipping straight from the can. In fact, many breweries that package their beer in cans encourage it. But if you prefer a glass, there's certainly no shame in that either. Simply ask your bartender or host.

HOW TO READ A BEER LABEL

Beer labels are often full of information that might mean either a little or a lot depending on what you're interested in. Here are some common terms and acronyms you might encounter, what they mean, and where to find them on your can or bottle.

BREWERY NAME This isn't always obvious. In English-speaking countries, it's often followed by the words "Brewery," "Brewing," or "Beer Company." On Belgian labels, you may see the term "Brouwerij" or "Brasserie," which simply means brewery—not a place where you get steak frites. On German labels, it may be "Brauerei."

BEER OR BRAND NAME Sometimes it's easy to confuse the name or brand of the beer with the name of the brewery. For example, in the US many people think that "Fat Tire" is a brewery rather than a specific beer made by New Belgium Brewing Company. Ditto "High Life" (made by MillerCoors) and "Shock Top" (brewed by Anheuser-Busch).

ABV This means alcohol by volume, a measure of how much alcohol is in the beer as a percentage of its overall volume. ABV isn't always on the label, but often you can make an estimate based on style (witbier will usually be around 5 percent ABV, while a double IPA or imperial stout will be 8 to 10 percent). Smartphone apps like Untappd or BeerMenus often provide this information.

OG AND FG OG (original gravity) indicates how much sugar was present in the wort before it fermented, while FG (final gravity) is a measure of how much sugar remains when fermentation is done. A much lower FG indicates a dry, crisp beer, while a high FG indicates that the beer may be sweet or malty.

DATE CODES As discussed in chapter 5, date codes indicating a packaged-on or "enjoy by" date are often printed on a beer's label, or stamped or laser-etched on the can or bottle itself.

OTHER INFORMATION You'll also notice most beer labels give the address of the brewery or bottler/packager, the net contents in volume, and a government warning or health advisory about the effects of alcohol. Some brewers also include allergy warnings, a history of the brewery, beer and food pairing ideas, tasting notes, and even suggested serving temperatures.

BEER STYLE Brewers almost always list the beer style on the label, as part of the name or explicitly on the label. Some European brewers, particularly ones in Belgium and Germany, won't necessarily list this, since the brewery may be synonymous with a style—this includes most Trappist producers like Orval and Rochefort, and some German breweries that specialize in a single beer.

IBU International Bitterness Units are a measure of bitterness in beer, reported as parts per million of isohumulone, the main bittering compound derived from hops. IBUs are sometimes reported on labels, but are becoming less common as extremely bitter beers give way to more aromatic ones.

SRM The Standard Reference Method is a beer color index. It's calculated via a complicated formula, but it's easy to understand. It ranges from roughly 2 to >40 corresponding to light to dark beers. A pale lager, witbier, or Berliner weisse (without added fruit or syrup) will be around 2, while an imperial stout will be 40 or greater. In between is IPA and pale ale (around 6), Vienna lager and amber ale (around 9-14), brown ale (around 2), and regular stout or porter (north of 25). SRM is sometimes listed, but in general the style will indicate how light or dark in color a beer will be.

BEER PACKAGING
BOTTLES AND CAN SHAPES

750 ML

500 ML

375 ML

750 ML BOTTLE

A standard for many Belgian beers, including saisons, lambics, gueuzes, krieks, and Flanders reds. These styles and imperial stouts, barleywines, and mixed culture sours are popular in the US.

500 ML BOTTLE

An in-between-sized bottle sometimes used for specialty beers, and particularly popular in Germany. Depending on strength, 500 ml bottles are great for sharing with a friend.

375 ML BOTTLE

A European-sized bottle that's roughly equivalent to 12 oz. Usually containing a special beer and often sold as individual bottles with a cork and cage closure.

16 OZ

16 OZ CAN

Also known as "tall boys," pint-sized cans are increasingly popular with craft drinkers in the US, especially for hoppy ales like American IPAs, double IPAs, and even imperial IPAs. Sold as singles or four-packs.

12 OZ

12 OZ

12 OZ CAN

Your typical Budweiser can, usually sold in six-, twelve-, or twenty-four packs. Recently, incredibly popular with American craft breweries.

12 OZ BOTTLE

The most common six-pack glass bottle. Usually brown glass, which protects the beer from UV rays (which cause "skunking"). Sometimes clear or green glass is used.

BEER BOTTLE CLOSURES

Get to know about the different types of covers that are keeping your beer sealed in the bottle.

CROWN CAP—A standard metal cap, usually with twenty-one "teeth" that result from the cap being crimped around the mouth of the bottle. Common on almost all bottled beers.

WAXED TOP—Special-release bottles sometimes contain a wax seal over the crown, a striking gesture that looks rad and impressive, especially if the wax drips to form tentacles down the curvature of the bottle. It's not only for looks, though—wax also forms a sealant that keeps oxygen out, making wax-sealed bottles especially fit for aging. To open, use a foil cutter—the knife-like part of a waiter's corkscrew—to slice the wax horizontally along the neck of the bottle just below the crown. Peel or chip back the wax. Once the crown is exposed, pop the top like you would any other bottle.

CORK AND CAGE—A method of sealing a beer bottle like a bottle of sparkling wine, with a fat-top cork and a wire "cage" that's twisted around the cork. Most common on 750 ml bottles, including some saisons, some sours, and imperial stouts. Lambics often play a riff on the cork and cage closure with a crown cap in place of a cage and a skinny rather than bulbous cork. These often require a corkscrew to open, since there is no exposed cork to grip.

Waxed tops add to the simple aged style of these brown ale bottles

DESIGN YOUR OWN BEER LABEL

For anyone fantasizing about jacking in the nine to five in favor of starting their own beer-brewing empire, a company image is a good place to start. Begin by designing your own beer label artwork masterpieces. Use Sharpies, crayons, or pens to start drawing up your style ideas.

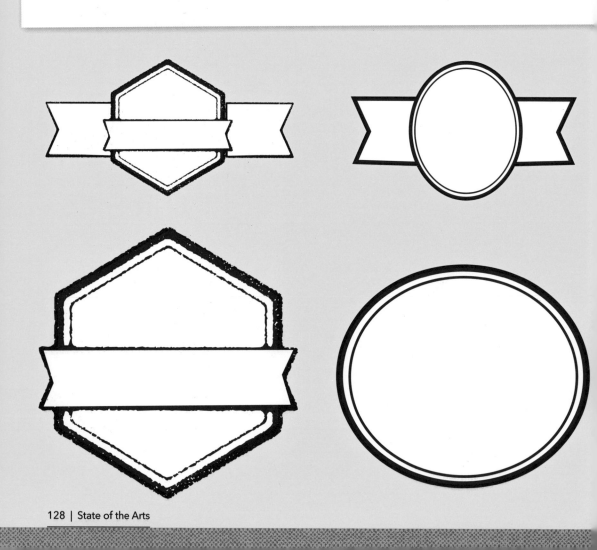

BEER QUEST!

We're going on a beer hunt! Here are three fun-filled beer trips throughout the world. Each includes stops with recommendations for regional specialties, breweries to visit, and styles to seek out. Be sure to have a dedicated sober driver for your journey or plan your trip around public transport and taxis, where you can. And contact breweries ahead of time to schedule your visit!

Get your boots on and head for a brewery

TRIP 1
UNITED STATES

SAN FRANCISCO–BEND–PORTLAND–SEATTLE
TOTAL MILES: *818*
TOTAL DRIVING TIME: *13 HOURS*
NUMBER OF DAYS: *4–5*

DAY 1 SAN FRANCISCO, CALIFORNIA

Start your journey in historic San Francisco. Anchor Brewing (1705 Mariposa Street) was founded here in 1896 and today, visitors can take walking tours followed by a tasting. Anchor is one of the few American breweries still producing the historic California common under its Anchor Steam label. Other specialties include Liberty Ale, one of the first examples of the American India pale ale, and Old Foghorn, the first American-style barleywine ever produced.

Next stop is Cellarmaker Brewing (1150 Howard Street), a hip, young brewery focused on small batches of hop-forward American-style IPAs and pale ales. The tasting room, with its exposed brick walls and industrial-chic light fixtures, is the perfect spot for sampling short pours of the brewery's ever-rotating selection of ales. Cellarmaker's barrel-aged beers include experimental saisons, porters, and stouts.

Next, you'll want to head across the bay to The Rare Barrel in Berkeley (940 Parker Street). This all-sour brewery was founded in 2011 and specializes in blending mixed-fermentation barrel-aged beers, many with additions of fruits and spices. The rustic tasting room is open Thursdays through Sundays and serves the brewery's own draft and bottled beers, as well as guest taps of non-sour beers from other California brewers.

Watch the sunset over the waterfront in Portland, Oregon

DAY 2 BEND, OREGON

The trek from San Francisco to Bend takes about seven and a half hours, much of it through scenic national forests. Your first stop will be Crux Fermentation Project (50 SW Division Street), a wood-paneled brewery, restaurant, and tasting room. The tasting room features more than twenty taps, all brewed on site, ranging from German-style Märzens and pilsners to regional Cascadian dark ales (AKA black IPA) and experimental IPAs.

Bend has an embarrassment of brewery riches and serious imbibers could spend several days exploring the city's goods. The original brewery that started it all, however, is Deschutes Brewery (1044 NW Bond Street). Deschutes has two Bend locations—a small tasting room at the production brewery in southwest Bend and a smaller brewery and pub in northwest Bend. Head to the latter for Deschutes classics like Black Butte Porter, Inversion IPA, and Fresh Squeezed IPA, as well as experimental and limited-release beers like gluten-free options, ciders, and rare barrel-aged ales.

Cap the day across the Deschutes River at 10 Barrel Brewing's original pub location (1135 NW Galveston Avenue). This brewery features more than a dozen beers on draft, including the flagship Apocalypse IPA and Sinistor Black Ale.

DAY 3 PORTLAND, OREGON

Today is a shorter drive to Portland—America's and the Pacific Northwest's premier beer city, with close to eighty-five breweries in the metro area. Start at Commons Brewery (630 SE Belmont Street), a Belgian farmhouse-inspired spot focusing on saisons. The bright, airy tasting room features thirteen taps ranging from the flagship Urban Farmhouse Ale to Flemish Kiss (a foeder-aged Brett ale) to Common Hazel (a California common brewed with hazelnuts). Skip one block east to Cascade Brewing where you'll find a treasure trove of barrel-aged fruit beers.

Next, head north to Great Notion Brewing (2204 NE Alberta Street) for dank IPAs and more barrel-aged beers. The tasting room focuses on juicy IPA more commonly found in the American Northeast than Pacific Northwest. Try Juice Box Double IPA,

a hazy hop bomb, and Double Stack Northwest Breakfast Stout, an imperial stout aged with Vermont maple syrup and roasted coffee beans.

Head back to Southeast Portland and stop in at Hair of the Dog (61 SE Yamhill Street), a PDX institution since 1993. The most famous beers are barleywine- and stock ale–style beers with huge aromas of dark fruit and chocolate.

NOTE: *IF YOU HAVE TIME, CHECK OUT: APEX, BAERLIC, BAILEY'S TAPROOM, BASECAMP, BELMONT STATION, BREAKSIDE BREWING, ECLIPTIC, EX NOVO, FAT HEAD'S, GREEN DRAGON, HOPWORKS URBAN BREWING, HORSE BRASS PUB, RACCOON LODGE, UPRIGHT BREWING, WIDMER BROTHERS, AND MORE.*

Seattle's *Fremont Troll*

DAY 4 SEATTLE, WASHINGTON

Hit the road north for the three-hour drive to Cloudburst Brewing (2116 Western Avenue) near Seattle's iconic Pike Place Market. This pint-sized brewery specializes in one-off batches of Northwest IPAs, saisons, and culinary-inspired beers like oyster stouts, a brown ale with cinnamon and raisins, and a Ricola cough drop–based ale with fourteen herbs and spices.

Then head northwest along the Puget Sound to Holy Mountain Brewing (1421 Elliott Ave W), a heavy metal–themed temple to beer. Many of the brewery's wood-fermented farmhouse ales are aged in foeders, barrels, and puncheons, and are on offer at the brewery's stark, minimalist tasting room. The ten drafts also include saisons, pilsners, hoppy pale ales, and imperial stouts. The brewery's forte is Brett-fermented blended ales conditioned on wood and in the bottle. Pick up rare bottles and growlers to go.

Finally, drop in on Fremont Brewing (1050 N 34th Street) in its namesake Fremont district of Seattle for a family-friendly urban beer hall vibe with plenty of tasty brews. The game here is hoppy pale ales like Universal Pale Ale and Interurban IPA, along with seasonals and barrel-aged one-offs. There are often special cask ales as well as free pretzels and house-made soda for the kids.

TRIP 2 GERMANY

Germany has any number of beer pilgrimages one could embark on across its expanse. But the four stops chosen here feature particularly unique brews that historically were rarely made outside of their hometowns. Let's go!

COLOGNE–BAMBERG–LEIPZIG–BERLIN
TOTAL MILES: *520*
TOTAL DRIVING TIME: *9 HOURS*
NUMBER OF DAYS: *4*

DAY 1 COLOGNE

In Germany, Kölsch can only be brewed in Cologne (Köln). And while you're in Cologne, pretty much the only beer available on draft at restaurants, bars, and clubs is Kölsch. The pale greenish-hued brew is often thought of as a lager-ale hybrid, but strictly speaking, it is a pale ale holdover from the pre-lager days of German brewing. Light in color and alcohol, it has a smooth, grassy flavor considerably less bitter than a pilsner, with a fruity, dry finish.

The quintessential place to try it is Brauerei Päffgen (Friesenstraße 64–66), just outside the old city center. This boisterous, wood-adorned tavern serves traditional unfiltered Kölsch dispensed from wooden barrels. Päffgen's beer has a remarkably fresh hop character. Order from the blue-clad, tray-toting waiters who sling Kölsch in its traditional tall, skinny, straight-walled 200 ml glasses. (Note: The brewery also runs the historic Gaststätte Lommerzheim, a traditional Kölsch pub that it purchased and reopened in 2008.)

For a taste of new German craft brewing, head to Braustelle (Christianstraße 2), Cologne's first craft brewpub. A fixture of the Ehrenfeld neighborhood, it attracts both locals and craft-beer tourists. The premier brew is Helios, Braustelle's take on its hometown beer. But also check out the brewery's more experimental ales like American-style pale ales, fruited sours, altbier (a style typical of Düsseldorf), and smoked barrel-aged stouts.

Finally, drop in on Gaffel Am Dom (Bahnhofsvorplatz 1), located adjacent to Cologne's massive Gothic cathedral. Gaffel is perhaps the hoppiest Kölsch in all of Cologne, with a sprightly bitterness. Check out the beautiful copper brewing equipment on display along the walls and the intricate stained-glass ceiling.

DAY 2 **BAMBERG**

Next, head to Franconia, the northern part of Bavaria, a region with easily one of the most interesting brewing cultures in all of Germany, if not the world. Franconia hosts more breweries per capita than any other part of Germany, and boasts robust pilsners and historic smoke-laced rauchbiers.

The finest rauchbiers are found in the middle of the historic city center where Schlenkerla is located (Dominikanerstraße 6). The brewery's taproom offers a variety of smoked malt beers, from the flagship Aecht Schlenkerla Rauchbier (with a Märzen-like base) to smoked wheat beers and seasonals. Depending on what time of year you're visiting, you may find specialties like fastenbier (a smoked bock-style beer brewed for Lent), kräusen (a blend of traditional and young smoked lager), or Christmas ale (a doppelbock brewed with oak-smoked rather than beechwood-smoked malt). All the beers are intensely flavored with smoke, lending them a medley of barbecued meat, Islay Scotch, and caramel malt flavors.

With the taste of smoke lingering on your tongue, head across the Regnitz River to Brauerei Spezial (Obere Königstraße 10) for even more rauchbier suds. Spezial is Bamberg's second rauchbier producer, but crafts smoked beers with a deft, gentle touch that doesn't overwhelm your palate the way Schlenkerla might. Spezial's range includes traditional lagers, Märzen, and wheat beer, as well as "Ungespündet" beer, an unfiltered, full-bodied lager that literally translates as "unbunged." The brewery houses an inn and restaurant—a one-stop shop for traveling beer nerds.

Your final stop should be at Mahrs Bräu (Wunderburg 10), one of the finest breweries in Franconia. This family-run establishment, with roots in the region dating back to 1895, boasts an old-world brewpub with traditional fare and a beer garden. Mahrs eschews the region's smoked beers in favor of traditional lagers and weissbiers. Also check out Mahrs Pilsner (a robust take on the style), Hell (an extremely light Helles lager), and Bock (a strong, velvety beer).

DAY 3 LEIPZIG

It's a three-hour drive north of Bamberg to Leipzig, the land of gose. If you wanted to visit the actual birthplace of the style, however, you would need to continue another two hours northwest to the historic town of Goslar. That's where gose was invented, on the banks of the tiny Gose River. By the early nineteenth century, the style was extremely popular in Leipzig—the exact reason it became synonymous with Leipzig is unclear—but had all but disappeared from Germany by World War II. Only since the 1980s has gose production appeared again, first in Leipzig and then back in Goslar.

Your first stop will be Ohne Bedenken (Menckestraße 5), a gosenschenke, or specialty gose bar, which closed for decades, but reopened in 1986 during gose's triumphant return to the city. This sprawling beer garden serves several varieties of gose, including Ritterguts, a brand made just outside Leipzig. The house gose is a slightly tart, highly refreshing thirst quencher of an ale made with wheat, salt, and coriander spice. Bartenders here will add schnapps and fruit syrups to dilute the tart bite, but opt for the beer straight, untainted by outside flavors. It's delicious and refreshing.

Another gose served at Ohne Bedenken is from a brewery a few miles south called Bayerischer Bahnhof (Bayrischer Pl. 1), a stop that should be next on your list to visit. The Bayerischer brewpub opened in a historic rail station in 2000 and now brews gose and several other styles right on premise. The brewery's Leipziger Gose is pale yellow in color with less sourness than Ritterguts and a more gentle mouthfeel and finish.

Finally, finish your day in Leipzig at Goldhopfen craft beer bar (Kolonnadenstraße 11), which has four taps of local beer and a handful of rare goses not commonly found elsewhere in the city.

Relax with a beer at Alexanderplatz, Berlin

DAY 4 BERLIN

Start your day at the admittedly touristy Alt-Berliner Weissbierstube (Rathausstraße 21), a cozy café specializing in the city's trademark, but nearly forgotten beer, Berliner weisse. Similar to gose, it is a light, refreshingly tart wheat ale soured with *Lactobacillus*. At Alt-Berliner, servers still dispense Berliner Weisse mit Schuss (with syrup) into customary wide-mouthed goblets with shots of sweet raspberry or woodruff syrup. Order it sans schuss for a true Berliner weisse experience.

Most of the Berliner weisse served at Alt-Berliner comes from the industrial Kindl brand. For a taste of old-school Berliner weisse made in small batches from authentic recipes, head to the Arminiusmarkthalle (Arminiusstraße 2–4). This sprawling food hall features lunch counters and a beer bar affiliated with Brewbaker, the makers of a lemony tart Berliner weisse first brewed in 2005.

Unlike Kindl, Brewbaker's Berliner is fermented with Brettanomyces, a traditional Berliner weisse method used to impart the beer with a complex, funky character.

Finally, wind north to Emil's Biergarten (Berliner Str. 80–82), where you'll find a plethora of beer options, including ones from Andreas Bogk and his Bogk-Bier Berliner Weisse. Bogk has been a well-known home brewer and roving professional brewer for years, but only recently laid down roots at the historic Willner Brauerei Berlin at the same address as Emil's in Pankow. Bogk's Berliner Weisse is made with a special strain of Brettanomyces that gave the original Berliner weisse its characteristic aroma.

MATCHING PAIRS

Based on what we hope is your *detailed* and *thorough* knowledge of this chapter—with strictly minimal use of finger-and-thumb bookmarks—in which of the following places are you most likely to find which of the following beer brands or types? Grab a pen and join them up.

WALLONIA	WEISSE
BEND	ARABIER
SEATTLE	FLEMISH KISS
LONDON	GUEUZE
BAMBERG	KÖLSCH
COLOGNE	RITTERGUTS
LEIPZIG	DEUCEBOX
PORTLAND	RICOLA COUGH-DROP ALE
BERLIN	OLD FOGHORN
FLANDERS	ORVAL
BRUSSELS	HELL
SAN FRANCISCO	INVERSION IPA

Solution on page 159

TRIP 3 BELGIUM

Belgium is divided into three regions: Wallonia in the south, Flanders in the north, and the capital, Brussels, in the center. Each has its distinct specialties when it comes to beer.

WALLONIA–BRUSSELS–FLANDERS AND BRUGES
TOTAL MILES: 275
TOTAL DRIVING TIME: 6 HOURS
NUMBER OF DAYS: 4

Cityscape in Wallonia

DAY 1 WALLONIA

It would be impossible to cover all of what Wallonia has to offer beer-wise in just one day, but the three spots offered here are a great start.

Begin in the far southeast of Belgium, at Abbaye d'Orval (Orval 1, Florenville). Although the monastery grounds date back to 1132, the present-day brewery was built in 1931. Orval makes just two beers: regular Orval, an amber-hued saison-like beer with Brettanomyces, and Petite Orval, a smaller version of that beer. Note that visitors cannot tour the brewery itself, but can visit the brewery museum.

Your next stop is 55 miles north to the Abbaye Trappiste de Rochefort in the town of Rochefort. Sadly, unlike Orval, the abbey does not allow visitors, but there are many bars and cafés within town in which to drink the local specialty. Drop in at La Gourmandise (Rue de Behogne 24) for local cheeses, cured meats, and Trappist beer. As well as the Rochefort trilogy—6, 8, and 10 (beers of

increasing strength)—try a Chimay, another Trappist brewery further afield in the region.

The small village of Soy is a thirty-minute drive from Rochefort. You'll need to call at least a few days ahead of visiting Fantôme Brasserie (Rue Préal 8, Soy). Dany Prignon, the sole proprietor, is a whimsical brewer who uses an ever-evolving variety of spices, herbs, and flowers in his special saisons. Fantôme saisons vary from fruity and light to robust, dark, and funky. One rumor is that Prignon doesn't even like his own beers; he prefers stronger Trappist ales and soft drinks instead!

DAY 2 BRUSSELS

Brussels is the home of lambic, perhaps the most unique and revered beer in the world. Your first stop should be Brasserie Cantillon and the neighboring Brussels Gueuze Museum (Rue Gheude 56). Brasserie Cantillon was founded around 1900 and is currently run by the great-grandson of founder Paul Cantillon, Jean Van Roy, who brews every ounce of beer the brewery producers. Onsite is a tasting room where lambic enthusiasts can taste rare vintages.

A short drive northwest is Brasserie de la Senne (Chaussée de Gand 565, Sint-Jans-Molenbeek). A small, artisanal brewery, de la Senne focuses on more modern beer styles like hoppy ales, while remaining dedicated to the traditional bold beers of Belgium (Note: The tasting room is closed on weekends.)

Finally, head back into central Brussels to Moeder Lambic Original (Rue de Savoie 68), a famed lambic and gueuze spot that is widely considered one of the best beer bars in the world. The menu

The *Mannekin-Pis* statue, Brussels

is heavy on rare and vintage gueuze and kriek, but also features an assortment of Trappist ales and saisons. A second location of Moeder is now open near the famous Manneken-Pis statue.

NOTE: *MANY BELGIAN BREWERIES ARE SMALL, FAMILY-RUN OPERATIONS THAT HOLD UNRELIABLE AND ERRATIC OPENING HOURS FOR THE PUBLIC. IT'S ALWAYS BEST TO CALL AHEAD TO SCHEDULE A VISIT DESPITE WHAT IS LISTED ON BREWERY WEBSITES OR IN TRAVEL LITERATURE.*

Delirium Nocturnum, Delirium Tremens, several Trappist Rochefort varieties

DAYS 3 AND 4 **FLANDERS AND BRUGES**

If you happen to depart Brussels for Flanders on a Sunday morning and are thirsty for even more lambic, be sure to stop by the pub In de Verzekering tegen de Grote Dorst (Frans Baetensstraat 45, Lennik). This traditional Pajotten café (whose name translates as "In the Insurance against Great Thirst") is a holdover from a bygone era when lambic ruled this part of Belgium. It features one of the largest and rarest selections of lambic, gueuze, and kriek in the world. The café is open only on Sundays, on official Church holidays, and whenever a funeral is being held at the adjacent St. Ursula Church. (Again, always call ahead before detouring out of your way, even if it is a Sunday.)

Flanders is home to a variety of beer styles, but the most iconic is Flanders red. The style is synonymous with Rodenbach, whose original brewery is located in the town of Roeselare (Spanjestraat 133). Dating back to 1821, the gorgeously preserved brewery is perfect for visiting (reserve ahead online or over the phone). Try the medium-tart red ales like Rodenbach Classic and Grand Cru (both blends of aged and new beer) or opt for the rare Alexander.

Your next stop is De Dolle Brouwers, a thirty-minute trip northwest in the town of Diksmuide (Roeselarestraat 12b). This small, artisanal brewery was founded in 1980 in a historic building with a brewing history dating back to the 1800s. De Dolle ("The Mad Brewers") makes some of the most aggressively flavored but balanced beer in West Flanders. Of note are the Arabier, a 9 percent ABV hoppy beer made with whole leaf hops from nearby Poperinge, and Oerbier Special Reserva, the brewery's take on the local oud bruin–style ale. Call ahead to schedule a visit and, if you visit around Christmastime, do not leave without a bottle of Stille Nacht Christmas ale.

NOTE: *IF YOU WANT TO VISIT ANOTHER MONASTERY, JUST HALF AN HOUR DRIVE SOUTH OF DE DOLLE IS WESTVLETEREN (DONKERSTRAAT 12, VLETEREN), PERHAPS THE MOST EXCLUSIVE OF ALL THE TRAPPIST BREWERS. BEER SALES ARE BY APPOINTMENT ONLY, YOU MUST RESERVE AHEAD ONLINE.*

Otherwise, head north to Bruges, the original capital of Flanders, where gruits were long the beverage of choice. In fact, many Flanders ales still contain a blend of herbs and spices, a modern-day reflection of the region's gruit tradition. Bruges has many options for beer lovers, including 't Brugs Beertje (Kemelstraat 5), a cozy but bustling bar near the city center with a menu of more than 300 beers organized by region. Nearby is Struise Brouwers Beer Shop (Burg 15), a tiny shop and bar specializing in beers from its parent brewery De Struise (located in Oostvleteren, near Westvleteren), as well as rare bottles from American and European brewers. Three draft beers are permanently available, alongside an ever-rotating selection.

A canal in Bruges, lined with Medieval houses, radiant at dusk

Several bars in town specialize in Trappist beers. Two of the best are Café Rose Red, located on the ground floor of the Hotel Cordoeanier (Cordoeanierstreet 18), and Le Trappiste (Kuipersstraat 33). A handful of other brewers in Bruges welcome visitors, including De Halve Maan (Walplein 26) and Bourgogne des Flandres (Kartuizerinnenstraat 6).

SATURDAYS AT LONDON'S BERMONDSEY BEER MILE

The current hotspot of London's modern brewing scene is located under a series of railway arches in the southeast neighborhood of Bermondsey. Five breweries are located along the trail and each Saturday they open their doors to the public, allowing beer-seeking adventurers to embark on a brewery crawl along the Bermondsey Beer Mile.

The neighborhood's DIY beer movement was sparked by the now-world-renowned The Kernel brewery, founded here in 2009. Others like Partizan, Brew by Numbers, Fourpure, and Anspach & Hobday have followed suit, imbuing the area with beery goodness.

Start south and work your way northwest. Your first stop will be Fourpure Brewing Co. (22 Bermondsey Trading Estate, Rotherhithe New Road, SE16 3LL), founded in 2013 by brothers Thomas and Daniel Lower. The name references the four "pure" ingredients in brewing: water, malt, hops, and yeast. The brothers utilize a twenty-barrel brewhouse to crank out fresh hoppy beers like Session IPA and Deucebox, an imperial IPA, as well as traditional British styles like oatmeal stout and barleywine.

Next up is Partizan Brewing (8 Almond Street, SE16 3LR), opened in 2012 by chef Andy Smith and former Redemption brewer Andy Moffat. The brewery focuses on dark ales like foreign-export stouts, barrel-aged imperial stouts, and black IPAs, as well as American-style pale ales and IPAs. They even collaborated with Denmark's Mikkeller on a barrel-aged Belgian-style quad ale.

A short walk away is The Kernel (Arch 11 Dockley Road Industrial Estate, SE16 3SF), which was founded by Evin O'Riordain. The Kernel is known for its dry-hopped American-style IPAs like Double Citra and Mosaic, and its ever-evolving selection of IPAs is rounded out with a variety of historically inspired stouts like Imperial Brown Stout London 1856 and Export Stout London 1890.

Next stop is Brew By Numbers (79 Enid Street, SE16 3RA). Co-founders Tom Hutchings and David Seymour were inspired by The Kernel's O'Riordain, as well as craft beer scenes in Australia and New Zealand. Their beers are named via a numerical system, which first lists style (01, 02, 03, etc.) and then iteration of that style (01/01, for example, is a saison with Citra hops, while 05/03 is an IPA with Amarillo and Mosaic).

Your final stop is Anspach & Hobday (118 Druid Street, SE1 2HH), a Kickstarter-funded brewery opened in 2014 by Jack Hobday and Paul Anspach. The duo focuses on dark ales like porters and stouts. Perhaps their most famous beer is Smoked Brown, a cross between a traditional brown ale and a German smoked rauchbier.

The Kernel brewery kickstarted south London's bustling beer movement

BEER GLOSSARY

ABBEY ALE Any beer made in a monastic brewery, brewed for a monastery, or brewed commercially and styled on traditional Trappist ales, most commonly dubbels, tripels, and quads.

ADJUNCT A supplemental unmalted grain or fermentable sugar—rice, corn, candi sugar, etc.—added to the mash in order to supplement the malt, lighten the beer's body, or to boost alcohol.

ALCOHOL The amount of alcohol in beer varies depending on the amount of fermentable sugars added during the mash.

ALE One of two main categories of beer, the other being lager.

AROMA HOPS These are used for their aromatic rather than bittering qualities and are generally considered "late-addition" hops—added near the end of the boil and/or as a dry-hop addition during fermentation and conditioning.

BARLEY A member of the grass family that grows in temperate climates. In its malted state, barley creates the base of nearly every beer brewed around the world.

BARLEYWINE Not wine at all, but a high-strength beer originally marketed as a competitor to dessert wines like port and sherry.

BARREL Used to age and, less commonly, ferment beer. They range in size from small casks to large-format puncheons. Most barrel-aged beers are conditioned in wood that once contained bourbon, whiskey, or wine.

BERLINER WEISSE A tart, refreshing wheat ale native to Berlin and once considered the Champagne of the North. Currently experiencing a revival in its namesake city and particularly in the US.

BIÈRE DE GARDE A malty, somewhat strong type of French farmhouse ale that literally translates as "beer for keeping." Closely related to saisons.

BITTERING HOPS So-called early-addition hops that are high in alpha acid content and used to add a bitter backbone to beer. Also used for their preservative qualities.

BOIL A step in the brewing process where wort is boiled inside the brew kettle. The wort is boiled to remove volatile compounds, and bittering hops are usually added during this phase.

BOTTLE-CONDITIONED A process of maturing and carbonating a beer in its final packaging (the bottle) with additional yeast and/or sugars.

BRETTANOMYCES A yeast strain brewers typically want to keep out of a beer, but sometimes used as a secondary or even primary fermenting strain.

BREW KETTLE A vessel used during the brew process in which wort is boiled and hops added.

CASK A small barrel used for aging, storing, and sometimes serving beer.

CICERONE A beer certification program akin to a wine sommelier. Levels include Certified Beer Server, Certified Cicerone, Advanced Cicerone, and Master Cicerone.

CRAFT (BEER AND BREWERY) A hotly debated term that nominally indicates a small, independent brewery not majority owned by an outside entity. The Brewers Association defines craft as "small, independent, and traditional," with a cap on production at six million barrels per year.

DRY HOPPING A brewing technique of adding hops late in the beer-making process to increase hop aroma without adding significant bitterness. Dry hops may be added to the cooled wort or beer during primary or secondary fermentation, or even later in the process.

DUBBEL A malty, moderately strong Belgian-style beer often brewed by Trappist and other monastic breweries, though also commonly brewed by commercial brewers in Belgium and the US.

FERMENTATION The metabolic process of converting sugars via yeast or bacteria to alcohol, gases, and acids. Fermentation is how beer gets its alcohol, natural carbonation, and many of the esters and acids that contribute to its final flavor.

FILTRATION Passing beer (or any liquid) through a permeable substance to remove solid matter in suspension, including hop debris and yeast.

FRESH HOP Fresh hop ales are made with just-harvested hops that haven't undergone drying or other processing. Adds huge but ephemeral aromas that dissipate quickly.

GLUTEN-FREE AND GLUTEN-REDUCED BEER Most gluten-free beers are made with sorghum, rice, buckwheat, or corn; those made with barley, wheat, or other grains that contain gluten are not considered gluten free. Gluten-reduced beers are brewed with malted barley, but treated with an enzyme to break down most of the glutens in the beer.

GOSE A tart German wheat ale brewed with coriander and salt.

GRUIT Beer made with bittering herbs and botanicals in place of hops—a style that predates hop beers.

GUEUZE A blended Belgian beer comprised of lambics of various ages, usually one, two, and three years old.

HEFEWEIZEN A wheat ale from Germany. Also known as weissbier and recognized for its banana and clove flavors.

HOPS The primary bittering agents in beer. They are the flowers of the plant *Humulus lupulus* and provide aromas, increased head retention, and shelf stability in beer.

IMPERIAL A descriptor for big, bold beers with an elevated ABV, usually around 10 percent ABV or higher.

INDEPENDENT BREWERY A vague term increasingly used to denote a brewery not owned by a parent company, umbrella group, or outside entity.

INDIA PALE ALE IPA is the most popular style of craft and independent beer in the world. It originated in the UK, but the Americanized version is its most favored iteration.

INTERNATIONAL BITTERNESS UNIT Abbreviated IBU, it's a measure of bitterness in beer.

LAGER A group of cold, bottom-fermenting beers that makes up one of two primary beer categories (the other being ale).

LAMBIC A type of beer specific to Brussels and environs made with raw wheat, aged hops, and fermented "spontaneously" by yeast and bacteria inoculated in an open-air environment. The base beer of gueuze, kriek, framboise, and other beers.

MACROBREWERY A big, industrial brewery producing many millions of barrels of beer a year. The term is used to distinguish between "microbreweries," craft breweries, or independent breweries.

MALT Refers to malted grain, which forms the base of nearly all beer (excluding gluten-free ones). Malting is a process in which grain is partially sprouted in order for fermentable sugars to be more readily available and more easily released during the brewing process.

MÄRZEN A darkish red lager native to Munich, but closely related to the Vienna lagers of Austria. Until the 1980s, it was the main beer served at Oktoberfest.

MASH The grain and possibly adjuncts used in the first step of the brewing process when hot water is used to extract fermentable sugars. A mash almost always includes a high proportion of malted barley and sometimes other grains like rice, corn, and wheat.

MOUTHFEEL A combination of physical and chemical sensations that combine to form textures, ranging from watery and insipid to velvety, thick, and coating. Mouthfeel is the culmination of specific sensations like dryness, astringency, warmth, and carbonation.

NANOBREWERY The smallest of small breweries often run by just one or two people making tiny batches of beer commercially. Used to distinguish the extremely small-scale production from even modest craft breweries and microbreweries.

NITROGEN Nitrogen gas is sometimes used in combination with carbon dioxide to dispense beer from a tap. These are called nitrogen or nitro drafts and are specific to only a handful of styles (like stouts). They impart a velvety mouthfeel and are slightly sweet, but dissipate aromas.

NOBLE HOPS These classic European hops have been grown in specific regions for centuries and are named for the regions where they were developed.

PILSNER A type of pale lager developed in the western Bohemian town of Plzeň in the Czech Republic, in the mid-nineteenth century. Now synonymous with German and Czech beer, the pilsner recipe is one of the most copied and widely brewed styles in the world.

PORTER The grandfather of many dark ales including stouts, these beers were popular among dockworkers and other laborers dating back centuries. The style is roasty and dark in color with moderate alcohol and a medium body.

QUAD A sweet, malty Belgian-style ale around 10 percent ABV and ruby to dark amber in color. Sometimes brewed in Trappist monasteries for Christmas and winter consumption.

RAUCHBIER A beer made with smoked malt. Can be practically any style, from pilsners and lagers to wheat ales and porters. Outside of Germany referred to as "smoke beer."

REINHEITSGEBOT Applies to all of Germany, but there are several different clauses and applications of the law depending on the type of beer, brewing location within Germany, and whether the market is domestic or export.

RYE A type of grain used to make certain beer styles. It adds a spicy dryness and a prickly mouthfeel to beer.

SAISON An effervescent "farmhouse" ale native to the Wallonia region of southern Belgium and northern France. Saison (which means "season") is a catchall category for various beers made throughout this region.

SCHWARZBIER A dark brown to black lager native to Germany.

SCOTCH ALE Native to Edinburgh, this malty, boozy beer is dark reddish in color, with hints of toffee, caramel, and dried fruit.

SESSION Refers to a highly drinkable, low-ABV beer that can be consumed one after another during a beer drinking "session."

SOUR ALE A catchall term referring to myriad styles of tart and acidic beers.

SPONTANEOUS FERMENTATION Refers to beer made with native ambient yeast and bacteria—that is, those occurring naturally in the air—rather than a pitched culture. Lambic is the prime example. Most use a coolship vessel for ambient inoculation.

STEAM BEER One of the few indigenous American beer styles, first brewed in California during the gold rush. Essentially a lager yeast beer fermented at higher-than-usual, ale-like temperatures.

STOUT An offshoot of porter, stouts are dark, roasty beers that range drastically in body and flavor from the dry stouts of Ireland (velvety smooth and around 4 percent ABV) to the modern-day imperial stouts of American (viscous, thick, and around 10 percent or higher ABV).

TERROIR A wine term that means flavors and tastes are imparted by the natural environment—soil, geography, and climate—in which the wine is grown. Beer rarely reflects terroir in the same way, but some noble hops can impart a particular terroir as well as ambient yeasts in lambic and other spontaneous beers.

TRIPEL A light-colored, Abbey-style ale with fruity esters and a medium body. Most are around 8 or 9 percent ABV and are well balanced with bitterness, sweetness, and maltiness all contributing to the overall taste.

VARIANT A base beer that's had some alteration to it, like barrel aging or an additional ingredient.

WET HOPS Nominally different to fresh hops, wet hops are undried, unprocessed hops that must be used within twenty-four hours of harvesting before oxidation and spoilage occur.

WILD ALE An imprecise term used to describe a beer made with a so-called wild yeast strain like Brettanomyces or fermented with additional bacteria like *Lactobacillus* or *Pediococcus*. (Ironically, most modern Brett and bacteria come from a laboratory, so they are anything but wild.)

WITBIER A hazy Belgian wheat ale typically spiced with coriander and orange peel. May also contain oats for a creamy, cloudy appearance and mouthfeel.

WORT The sugary substance resulting from combining hot water and grain. Also known as unfermented beer.

YEAST Yeast are the primary microorganisms responsible for fermentation in beer. Most beer is fermented with a strain of Saccharomyces yeast, but Brettanomyces is occasionally used for certain beers.

FESTIVALS AND FUN

JANUARY

RATEBEER BEST: Santa Rosa, California, US. A daylong festival featuring beers from rare and cult brewers from around the world; the highest-rated breweries on the RateBeer website are present— and there's an awards ceremony where brewers are honored over a special dinner. (ratebeerbest.com)

FEBRUARY

EXTREME BEER FESTIVAL: Boston, Massachusetts, US. A gathering of strange and esoteric brews that are "extreme" in their processes and approach. Run by Beer Advocate. (beeradvocate.com/extreme)

MARCH

HUNAHPU'S DAY: Tampa, Florida, US. Cigar City Brewing throws a huge daylong festival to celebrate the release of Hunahpu's imperial stout. The festival is the capstone event of the annual Tampa Bay Beer Week. (hunahpusday.com)

APRIL

DE NACHT VAN DE GROTE DORST ("THE NIGHT OF GREAT THIRST"): Eizeringen, Belgium. A biennial lambic festival that's produced in association with the lambic pub In de Verzekering tegen de Grote Dorst. Attendance is free, but visitors must purchase tokens, which are exchanged for pours from dozens of producers. (geuzegenootschap.be/en/the-night-of-great-thirst)

MAY

PHILLY LOVES BEER: Philadelphia, Pennsylvania, US. A weeklong celebration of beer; highlights not just local producers, but also welcomes producers from around the country. (phillylovesbeer.org)

MIKKELLER BEER CELEBRATION: Copenhagen, Denmark. Attracting some of the best brewers from all over the world, the focus is heavily on hoppy American beer styles, imperial stouts, and traditional Belgian ales like lambics, saisons, and gueuze. (mikkeller.dk)

JUNE

SAVOR: Washington, DC, US. The Brewers Association throws this beer-and-food-pairing soirée every year, matching eighty-five of America's best breweries with chefs from around the US and small-bite plates. (savorcraftbeer.com)

JULY

OREGON BREWERS FESTIVAL: Portland, Oregon, US. A five-day extravaganza of Oregon-made brews. Each participating brewer brings one beer to pour—there are often more than one hundred different beers available. (oregonbrewfest.com)

Celebrate beer all year long at this selection of festivals throughout the world.

Celebrate beer with fellow enthusiasts

AUGUST

GREAT TASTE OF THE MIDWEST: Madison, Wisconsin, US. Features more than 150 of the Midwest's best independent brewers at Olin Park overlooking Lake Monona in downtown Madison. (greattaste.org)

GREAT BRITISH BEER FESTIVAL (AKA GBBF): London, UK. Organized by the Campaign for Real Ale (CAMRA) during the first full week of August, from Tuesday to Saturday. Has nearly a thousand international beers and features the Champion Beer of Britain awards. (gbbf.org.uk)

SEPTEMBER

OKTOBERFEST: Munich, Germany. The most famous beer festival in the world, this two-week blowout is held every mid-September, extending into the first weekend in October. The festival strictly regulates what beer can be served here—it must be from one of the large breweries that brew inside the city of Munich, and the primary beer served is called festbier. (oktoberfest.de)

OCTOBER

GREAT AMERICAN BEER FESTIVAL (AKA GABF): Denver, Colorado, US. More than 800 breweries participate in this three-day festival, and well over 8,000 beers are entered into a competition that has more than eighty categories. GABF also features the Paired festival, which matches a handful of

exclusive beers with upscale food from highly acclaimed chefs. (greatamericanbeerfestival.com)

THE FESTIVAL: Louisville, Kentucky, US. Also known as the Shelton Brothers Fest, this specialty beer festival is put on by American beer importer Shelton Brothers. The main draw is the company's portfolio of rare and esoteric beers, all poured under one roof. (sheltonbrothers.com/festival)

NOVEMBER

FESTIVAL OF WOOD- AND BARREL-AGED BEERS: Chicago, Illinois, US. This big beer festival attracts more than 150 breweries every year, pouring close to 500 different strong beers. It also features an accompanying awards ceremony. (fobab.com)

FURTHER READING

SUBSCRIBE TODAY!

The following magazines about beer are worth reading:

ALL ABOUT BEER (allaboutbeer.com)
BEER ADVOCATE MAGAZINE (beeradvocate.com/mag)
BEER & BREWER (beerandbrewer.com)
BEER MAGAZINE (camra.org.uk)
BREW YOUR OWN (byo.com)
DRAFT MAGAZINE (draftmag.com)
IMBIBE MAGAZINE (imbibemagazine.com)
ØLENTUSIASTER (ale.dk)
ZYMURGY (homebrewersassociation.org)

LIBRARY OF BREWS

Want more information about beer styles, pairing food and beer, or becoming an expert taster? Check out these titles:

THE BEER BIBLE by Jeff Alworth
COMPLETE IPA by Josh Bernstein
FOOD & BEER by Daniel Burns and Jeppe Jarnit-Bjergsø
THE NEW WORLD GUIDE TO BEER by Michael Jackson (It's also worth seeking out Jackson's others books, including *Great Beers of Belgium, Beer Companion, Great Beer Guide,* and *Ultimate Beer.*)
TASTING BEER by Randy Mosher
THE OXFORD COMPANION TO BEER edited by Garrett Oliver
THE COMPLETE JOY OF HOMEBREWING by Charlie Papazian

A WEB OF KNOWLEDGE

There is a plethora of great beer content online, so log on to these sites:

BEERADVOCATE (beeradvocate.com)
BREWBOUND (brewbound.com)
THE FULL PINT (thefullpint.com)
GOOD BEER HUNTING (goodbeerhunting.com)
PRO BREWER (probrewer.com)
RATEBEER (ratebeer.com)
TAPS (tapsmagazine.com)

BEERS AND APPS

These smartphone apps will help you find specific beers near you and help you connect with other beer enthusiasts:

BEERMENUS—a website and smartphone app that allows users to search for specific beers on draft and in bottle shops nearby.
TAPHUNTER—a smartphone app for searching particular beers and finding what's on tap at bars, breweries, and restaurants around you.
UNTAPPD—a social networking and drinking app that allows users to check into beers while providing notes, ratings, reviews, and photos of the beer.

ORGANIZATIONS

These organizations help promote the good beer cause:

BEER JUDGE CERTIFICATION PROGRAM (BJCP) (bjcp.org)
BREWERS ASSOCIATION (brewersassociation.org)
CAMRA (Campaign for Real Ale) (camra.org.uk)
CICERONE (cicerone.org)

ACKNOWLEDGMENTS

Many, many thanks to Rica Dearman, Caroline Elliker, Sorrel Wood, Mark Searle, and everyone else at Quarto. To Dani Segelbaum, Nick Davies, and Jennifer Murphy at HarperCollins.

IN NEW YORK: Thanks to Augie Carton, John Holl, and Brian Casse at Steal This Beer podcast. To Jimmy Carbone, the Heritage Radio Network, and Roberta's for the weekly hangs. To Josh Bernstein, Niko Krommydas, and Aaron Goldfarb for professional support.

To Colin Whitlow, Jessica Walker, Aaron Barr, Chris Konya, Lucas Hearl, and Sara Kim for being my Abingdon contingent in Brooklyn. To Leslie Claiborne and Chris Townley for holding down the fort. To Emelia and Michael at Thirst for all the great wine.

To Peter Meehan and everyone at *Lucky Peach* (RIP). To Ben Keene and the crew at *BeerAdvocate* magazine. To Marian Bull at *GQ*. To Talia Baiocchi at *PUNCH*.

FURTHER AFIELD: To Luke Schmuecker in California for always being a phone call away when I need to moan and complain. To Matt Coats in Portland for making everything look good and forever cracking me up.

To Alex Smith, D. G. Owens, Dave French, Evan Bowles, and Harvey Clark for everything under the sun—you mean the world.

Beer writer Justin Kennedy

To Peggy and Joe Kennedy, teetotalers both, for the constant, steadfast support, no matter what. And to Jason, my brother—this is for you; forever and ever, amen.

Most of all to Laura Ball and Cleo Love Kennedy for your love and patience— the late nights, crowded fridges, endless wanderings, and massive weekly recycling hauls. You are everything. Cure CF!

BEER INDEX

CREDITS

t = top, b = bottom, l = left, r = right, tl = top left, tr = top right, bl = bottom left, br = bottom right, ml = middle left

4Corners: Adwo 141t

Alamy: Cultura Creative (RF) 3–5, 82–83; artstock 8–9; North Wind Picture Archives 10t; Alko 17; INTERFOTO 18; Alan King engraving 19; Loop Images Ltd 22–23; BigTom 23t; Cephas Picture Library 23, 25bl; Horizons WWP/TRVL 24m; Patti McConville 32; Marc Tielemans 33l; RealFood 34b; Mira 36l, 67; Marina Lvova 36r; Tribune Content Agency LLC 37; Robert Estall photo agency 48; Jeffrey Pickthall 51t; Reciprocity Images Editorial 52b; Craft Beer Photography 56b; Loop Images Ltd 63; Vaclav Mach 65; Ryan McGinnis 66; Lucas Vallecillos 70; George Fisher 75; Quagga Media 81t; Steve Cukrov 81b; Maurice Savage 84; Westend61 GmbH 87; RubberBall 88t; Hero Images Inc. 95; Will Stanton 97; Viktor Fischer 98; Beth Dixson 105t; PhotoAlto sas 106; Bon Appetit 111; Cristian M. Vela 121; George Fisher 127; RGB Ventures/SuperStock 134; Anna Stowe Travel 143tr; StockPhotosArt—Abstract 144–5; George Fisher 145l; Kathy deWitt 145r; MaZvone/Stockimo 160

Getty: Lori Epstein 7; Bert Hardy 20; Hulton Deutsch 25t; Matej Divizna/Contributor 53t; Ryan Pierse 121l; Samere Fahim Photography 140

iStock: RBOZUK 11; stock_colors 14; Pogonici 16–17; NatashaBreen 16; venemama 25br; User2547783c_812 31; LPETTET 32–33; BrilliantEye 40; MartinM303 42–43; mycola 47; querbeet 48–49; woolzian 54b; rudchenko 59br; Ken Rygh 60–61; Grafner 60; IakovKalinin 68–69; MishaKaminsky 72–73, 74; RuslanDashinsky 79b; Nic_Taylor 85bl; Gewoldi 85r; rasilja 86; akinshin 86, 96t, 97; GeorgeDolgikh 93r; ansonsaw 94t; supermimicry 98–99; chictype 104; Pogonici 105; VadimZakirov 107t; FotografiaBasica 111; futureimage 112; Jonathan Austin Daniels 113; wacomka 114; OlgaMiltsova 117; SQ_Studio 121r; MBPROJEKT_Maciej_Bledowski 130–1; Rachel Gulotta Photography 130; subjug 131, 132, 133, 134, 140, 141, 142 (pin); Paperkites 131, 132, 133, 134, 135, 136–7, 138, 141, 142 (string); arsenisspyros 132–3, 134, 140–1, 142–3 (cork board); LucianoBibulich 135, 136–7, 138; Nikada 138; Rouzes 150–1; VladOrlov 151

Shutterstock: kzww 1; KariDesign 2–3; Es sarawuth 35 (can); antoninaart 60–61t, 150–1t; CCat82 69b; Yurchenko Iryna 103; Kitch Bain 110; Jane Rix 127

Stocksy: Alexey Kuzma 35; LIOR + LONE 55t; SEAN LOCKE 74; Jelena Jojic Tomic 102; Sherry Heck 115t; Jelena Jojic Tomic 117b; Kevin Russ 132–3; Inigo Cia Da Riva 143tr

Illustrations: Tyler Gross 4–5, 15t, 24b, 30t, 34t, 46, 47t, 50b, 55b, 61, 69t, 88b, 100–101, 117t, 126, 142-3, internal stickers; Greg Stobbs/Squirlart 12, 28; Jason Anscomb, Rawshock Design 49, cover sticker; Karen Hood 64–5, 96; www.thescribbler.co.uk 21, 50t, 52t, 54t, 56t, 57t, 58t, 59t; original illustrations by Skatin Chinchilla 22, 33r, 71, 73, 80, 87t, 93, 94b, 99, 105b, 107b, 115b, 136–7b, 139; Leigh@KJA Artists 89

Breweries: Brian Casse/Carton Brewing 13; Shelton Brothers Imports 27; Mikkeller 29, 76–7; Cigar City Brewing 42; HonestBrew 46tr, 57b; Alesmith 30b; Evil Twin 31, 39; Off Color 38; Hair of the Dog 43; Oskar Blues 46tl; Fonta Flora 46ml; New Belgium Brewing 46bl; Founders Brewing Co. 51bl; Bell's Brewery 51br; De Dolle Brouwers 53b; Cellarmaking Brewing Co 58l; Modern Times Beer 58br; Braxton Brewing Co 97b, 124–5; Bitter Old Fecker Rustic Ales 118; LIC Beer Project 119; Gustav Karlsson Frost 120

Also: Marc Olivier Le Blanc 6; Bison Beer and Emma Donaghy 14b; Allagash Brewing Company 26; Louie Londt 45, 46br, 79, 85, 90–91, 92, 118–19, 122–3, 124–5, 141b, 157; back cover, endpapers; Photo © Brewers Association 108–109; Matt Coats 153

Quintet Publishing would also like to thank Bison Beer Crafthouse bottle store in Brighton, UK, for their assistance throughout the project, and experts Lottie Norton and Kai Wilton Ali who chose the sticker scents.

While every effort has been made to credit photographers, Quintet Publishing would like to apologize should there have been any omissions or errors, and would be pleased to make the appropriate correction for future editions of the book.

PUZZLE SOLUTIONS

PAGE 28 BREWDOKU

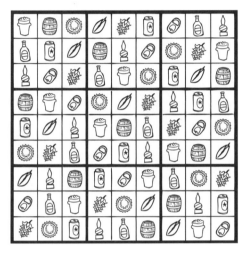

PAGE 64–65 HOP QUIZ!

1. b)
2. c)
3. a)
4. c)
5. b)
6. a)
7. c)
8. a)
9. Hemp and marijuana
10. Aroma, bittering, and dual-purpose
11. Activated at high temperatures
12. 45 degrees
13. Hop cone resin
14. Aroma
15. Cocoa
16. Oregon State University

PAGE 96 GRAINS OF TRUTH

1. False
2. False
3. True
4. False—they are among the worst!
5. True
6. False
7. True
8. False
9. False
10. True
11. True
12. False—they just cause those aromas to dissipate
13. False—it's more like 40°F
14. True
15. False—it's *much* safer with cans!

PAGE 116 WHICH BEER AM I?

1. Fortified beer
2. Pilsner—light lager also accepted
3. Saison—farmhouse ale also accepted
4. Irish stout
5. IPA
6. Trappist or Abbey ale
7. Imperial stout
8. Brown ale
9. Witbier—hefenweizen also accepted

PAGE 139 MATCHING PAIRS

(Alphabetically by place):
Bamberg/Hell; Bend/Inversion IPA; Berlin/weisse; Brussels/gueuze; Cologne/Kölsch; Flanders/Arabier; Leipzig/Ritterguts; London/Deucebox; Portland/Flemish Kiss; San Francisco/Old Foghorn; Seattle/Ricola cough-drop ale; Wallonia/Orval